Landmarks of world literature

Louis-Ferdinand Céline

JOURNEY TO THE END OF THE NIGHT

Landmarks of world literature

General Editor: J. P. Stern

LOUIS – FERDINAND CÉLINE

Journey to the end of the night

JOHN STURROCK

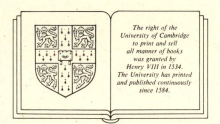

*The right of the
University of Cambridge
to print and sell
all manner of books
was granted by
Henry VIII in 1534.
The University has printed
and published continuously
since 1584.*

CAMBRIDGE UNIVERSITY PRESS

Cambridge
New York   Port Chester
Melbourne   Sydney

Published by the Press Syndicate of the University of Cambridge
The Pitt Building, Trumpington Street, Cambridge CB2 1RP
40 West 20th Street, New York, NY 10011, USA
10 Stamford Road, Oakleigh, Melbourne 3166, Australia

First published 1990

Printed in Great Britain at
the University Press, Cambridge

British Library cataloguing in publication data
Sturrock, John
Louis-Ferdinand Céline: journey to the end of the
night. – (Landmarks of world literature).
1. Fiction in French. Celine, Louis-Ferdinand, 1894–1961
I. Title   II. Series
843′.912

Library of Congress cataloging in publication data
Sturrock, John.
Louis-Ferdinand Céline, Journey to the end of the night / John
Sturrock.
      p.   cm. – (Landmarks of world literature)
ISBN 0–521–37250–X. – ISBN 0–521–37854–0 (pbk.)
1. Céline, Louis-Ferdinand, 1894–1961. Voyage au bout de la nuit.
I. Title.   II. Series.
PQ2607.E834V6385   1990
843′.912 – dc20   89–22284 CIP

ISBN 0 521 37250 X hard covers
ISBN 0 521 37854 0 paperback

Contents

Preface

Journey to the End of the Night is an 'autobiographical' novel. Its hero and narrator, Bardamu, travels to places and shares in punishing experiences which the novelist himself had travelled to or endured in the years before he became a writer. But an 'autobiographical' novel is not an autobiography, and we must not read the *Journey* as if it were an exotic kind of reportage, the more engaging as a narrative for being somehow 'true'. Bardamu tells his story in the first person but he is a 'character' in it, he is not the author speaking artlessly in his own person. Bardamu is not Céline, nor is the *Journey* the story of a part of Céline's life. However, both the hero and the plot of the book relate in interesting ways to particular facts in their author's biography, and for that reason the present study starts with a chapter which measures Céline's fiction against known, public fact. The comparison makes clear the strange nature of the misrepresentations of his life to be found in the *Journey*. This is a novel which becomes even more compelling once one has understood the deep perversity of temperament of the man who wrote it.

There is, though, a great deal more to Céline than temperament, perverse or otherwise; he is also an artist, and a self-conscious one. Indeed, this essay on the *Journey* argues a case, that it is a novel entirely of the modern age in the sophistication of its means. The main chapter analyses Céline's text with a view to identifying its most insistent, which are not always its most obvious themes, and to demonstrating also how surprisingly many moments it contains when the novelist dramatises not life as such but the processes of his own imagination. At one time, an approach to Céline such as this would have seemed eccentric, for so scathing is his prose that people for long saw him as an inescapably spontaneous writer, driven by strong feeling and with little time for reflection. I am not claiming here that he is an intellectual novelist because he is not; I am claiming that the text of the *Journey* is the work of someone who wrote with enormous care and high self-awareness: who for all his sound and fury is a thoroughly, brilliantly *literary* figure.

Céline belongs now definitively to literature, and no longer to politics, though for many years after 1938 he seemed to have abandoned the first for the second. In the later 1930s he became the most clamant and reckless of anti-Semitic writers in France, and during the war was accused of having collaborated or at least sympathised with the Nazis. For this he was sentenced in the courts but later amnestied. He was not, though, forgiven for his anti-semitism; his infamous pamphlets have never been republished, and there are those who still play down or even ostracise Céline the novelist because of them. This is to take his punishment too far. In the *Journey* there is only one momentary flash of anti-semitism – when, weirdly, the Jews are implicated, along with Blacks and 'Saxons', in having originated the new 'degenerate' dance music of 1915 – so it is not a question needing to be dealt with in an analysis of the novel. Very high claims may be made for Céline as a writer irrespective of his serious delinquency as a human being.

For their timely help with different sections of this book I thank two friends in the University of London: Professor Madeleine Renouard of Birkbeck College and Professor Douglas Johnson of University College, whose advice was both necessary and reassuring. The English versions of passages quoted from the *Journey* are my own. They are followed by page references to the French text which I have used, that edited by Henri Godard for the Bibliothèque de la Pléïade (marked P), and to the better and more recent of the two available English translations of the novel, that made by Ralph Manheim (New York: New Directions, 1983, marked M).

Chronology

	Céline's life	Historical and cultural events
1886		Edouard Drumont, *La France juive*.
1892		Edouard Drumont launches anti-semitic paper, *La Libre Parole*.
1894		Arrest and trial of the Jewish army captain Dreyfus, sentenced to be deported to Devil's Island, for treason.
1897		Emile Zola's *J'Accuse*, an open letter accusing the military authorities of having convicted Dreyfus wrongly. The 'Dreyfus Affair' is launched and divides society into anti-semites and anti-militarists. Maurice Barrès's *Les Déracinés* makes him the spokesman of a passionate new nationalism.
	C. born, in Courbevoie, in NW suburbs of Paris. Real name, Louis-Ferdinand Auguste Destouches.	
	Destouches family moves into central Paris.	Dreyfus retried, reconvicted, but immediately pardoned.
1899	Mother takes over shop selling 'novelty goods' in the Passage Choiseul, an arcade near the Opéra.	
1900		The Exposition Universelle opens in Paris, celebrating modernity, industrialisation etc, everything that C. came to hate.
1903		Urbain Gohier, *Le Peuple du XXe siècle, voyage aux Etats-Unis*, highly enthusiastic about the vitality and *chic* of American women. Gohier was later to publish a number of anti-semitic works.
1904	Death of his maternal grandmother, Céline Guillou, his favourite relative, whose first name he was later to take as his writer's alias.	

1905	First publication, in Russia, of the *Protocols of the Elders of Zion*, purporting to be an account of a Jewish plot to overthrow Christianity, later exposed as a forgery confected by the secret police.
1906	Dreyfus's conviction finally quashed.
1907	C. takes school-leaving certificate and is sent to Germany for a year to learn German.
1908	*L'Action française* launched as a daily paper of the extreme, anti-democratic right, by Charles Maurras and Léon Daudet.
1909	Sent to England, to two schools in Kent, to learn English.
1910	Starts work as a shop-boy, first in Paris, then in Nice.
1911	The 'Agadir Incident', gunboat diplomacy between Germany and France, foreshadowing 1914.
1912	Faced with conscription, C. joins the cavalry on a three-year engagement. Starts keeping a notebook of his (painful) experiences, published in 1965 as 'Carnet du cuirassier Destouches'.
1913	Poincaré becomes President of France. First volume of Marcel Proust's *A la recherche du temps perdu* published. Alain-Fournier, *Le Grand Meaulnes*.
1914	In action in Flanders, as a sergeant. Wounded in the arm carrying despatches, awarded Médaille Militaire and hospitalised in Paris.	Outbreak of First World War. German armies threaten Paris.

1915	Posted to London, to work in the French consulate. Frequents the docklands, Soho's underworld and the music-halls, all later to feature in the two parts of *Guignol's Band*.	
1916	Goes to French Cameroons, as an 'overseer' with a forestry company. Starts writing seriously: poems, a translation of Kipling and a short story, 'Des Vagues'.	Henri Barbusse, *Le Feu*, influential anti-war novel. Sigmund Freud, *Introduction to Psychoanalysis*.
1917	Returns to France for health reasons. Works for a publisher and for a popular science journal, *Eurêka*, a 'Review of Inventions'.	Bolshevik Revolution in Russia.
1918	Taken on by Rockefeller Foundation, and tours Britanny, lecturing on the prevention of tuberculosis.	Armistice agreed. Georges Duhamel, *Civilisation*. Oswald Spengler, *The Decline of the West*.
1919	Takes *baccalauréat* as a mature student, enrols as a medical student in Rennes, and marries Edith Follet, daughter of the Director of the Medical School there.	Peace Treaty of Versailles.
1920		League of Nations formed by signatories to Versailles Treaty, to work for international cooperation. Romain Rolland, *Colas Breugnon*.
1922	Continues medical studies in Paris, in hospitals and, unoffically, at the Institut Pasteur.	James Joyce, *Ulysses*.
1924	Submits his doctoral thesis, an impassioned account of the work of the nineteenth-century pioneer of antisepsis, Semmelweis. Joins the medical services of the League of Nations in Geneva.	
1925	First visit to the United States, leading party of doctors. Brief factory visits to Detroit and Pittsburgh, both exploited in *Voyage au bout de la nuit*.	Abel Gance, *Napoléon*, first (silent film) version. Joseph Conrad's *Heart of Darkness* translated into French.

1926	Travels on behalf of the League of Nations. Divorced by Edith Follet. Starts writing a play, *L'Eglise*, set in Africa, US and Geneva. Meets Elizabeth Craig, a young American dancer who joins him; to become the eventual dedicatee of *Voyage au bout de la nuit*.	Henry de Montherlant, *Les Bestiaires*. André Malraux, *La Tentation de l'Occident*. Louis Aragon, *Le Paysan de Paris*.
1927	Tries unsuccessfully to get *L'Eglise* published. Starts on a second play. Sets up as a GP in Clichy.	André Gide, *Voyage au Congo*. Sigmund Freud's *Essais de psychanalyse* published in French. Paul Morand, *Le Voyage*, explaining the new love of travel by the traumas of 1914–18 war.
1928	Starts publishing on questions of public health.	
1929	Becomes a locum at a working-class clinic in Clichy, and takes another part-time job with a pharmaceutical laboratory, writing their advertisements. Begins writing *Voyage au bout de la nuit* in his spare time.	Eugène Dabit, *Hôtel du Nord*, successful populist novel, written in a proto-Celinian 'spoken' French. Wall Street crash inaugurates world-wide depression. Erich Maria Remarque, *All Quiet on the Western Front*, powerful antiwar novel.
1930		Paul Morand, *New York*, a book in celebration of the United States which C. saw as 'jazzing up' the French language. Georges Duhamel, *Scènes de la vie future*, another, less enthusiastic account of American life.
1932	Death of father, Fernand Destouches. MS finally accepted for publication, and published in October. Narrowly fails to win the Prix Goncourt. Furore over the novel's often scabrous subject-matter and the duplicities of the prize jury make both C. and his novel celebrated. Wins the Prix Renaudot.	
1933	C's play; *L'Eglise*, is published, on the strength of the huge success of the *Voyage*.	Hitler takes power in Germany. Reichstag fire is followed by first Nazi persecution of German Jews. André Malraux, *La Condition humaine*.

1934	English translation of the *Voyage* published. C. in American, negotiating film rights and trying to persuade Elizabeth Craig to return to live with him.	Anti-parliamentary riots in Paris, led by rightwing groups. Henry Miller, *Tropic of Cancer*.
1935		Italian troops invade Abyssinia.
1936	Publication of C's second great novel, *Mort à credit* (*Death on the Instalment Plan*), to some acclaim, some dismay at its idiosyncratic style and much outrage at its outspokenness. C. visits USSR and on his return writes a pamphlet, *Mea Culpa*, to express his ferocious dislike of the country and its regime. Begins writing an 'army' novel, *Casse-pipe*, published only fragmentarily, after his death.	Rhineland remilitarised by Hitler. Popular Front coalition of the left forms government, under Blum. Vast wave of strikes. André Gide, *Retour de l'URSS*, expressing his deep disappointment with the Soviet Union. Charlie Chaplin, *Modern Times*.
1937	Publication of C.'s first major pamphlet, *Bagatelles pour un massacre*, scathing, pacifist, but above all ragingly anti-semitic. C. seen for the first time as an extreme ally of the political right.	Grande Exposition in Paris, echoing that of 1900. Jean Renoir, *La Grande illusion*, anti-war film.
1938	Second, equally anti-semitic pamphlet, *L'Ecole de Cadavres*. C.'s extremism isolates him, being reviled by the left and suspected by the right as a parody.	Munich agreement signed, between France, Britain and Germany, J.-P. Sartre, *La Nausée*, with an epigraph taken from C. Georges Bernanos, *Les grands cimetières sous la lune*.
1939	C. becomes ship's doctor on a troopship in the Mediterranean.	World War Two starts, with German invasion of Poland. Marcel Carné, *Le Jour se lève*.
1940	Goes to work at a clinic in Sartrouville, NW of Paris. Joins the exodus of refugees to the South-west, after the defeat, with an ambulance unit.	May–June. French armies routed. Germans occupy northern two thirds of France. Pétain government set up in Vichy.
1941	Publication of the third and final pamphlet, *Les Beaux draps*, a bitter diatribe against French degeneracy. Works as doctor in Bezons.	Germans invade Soviet Russia. Japanese attack on Pearl Harbor brings United States into the war.

1942	Brief trip to Berlin, in an attempt to transfer money to Denmark. Starts writing *Guignol's Band*, provisionally titled 'English Bar'.	Allied armies invade North Africa. Germans occupy southern France. Marcel Aymé, *Le Passe-Muraille*, a collection of stories by one of C.'s close friends and sympathisers.
1943	Marries Lucette Almanzor, a dancer and his regular companion since 1936.	Formation of the Milice, a paramilitary force intended to help the occupying Germans to counter the Resistance.
1944	First volume of *Guignol's Band* published. C. fears for his life as the liberation of France begins. Leaves with Lucette for Germany. Stops in Baden-Baden, Berlin, and finally Sigmaringen, the southern castle then sheltering members of the Pétain regime.	June. Allied forces land in Normandy, and then in southern France. Paris liberated. The *épuration* or purge of collaborationists begins. Marcel Carné, *Les Enfants du paradis*.
1945	Death of C.'s mother in Paris. Flight from Sigmaringen to Copenhagen through devastation of Germany. Warrant for C.'s arrest on charges of treason issued in Paris. In December, arrested by Danish authorities, in response to requests from France. C. spends eleven months in prison in Copenhagen.	Germany surrenders. Pétain tried and sentenced to death for treason. Sentence reduced to life imprisonment by General de Gaulle. Atomic bombs dropped on Japan. Suicide in prison of the writer Pierre Drieu La Rochelle, accused of collaboration. Execution of another rightwing writer, Robert Brasillach, and the Vichy minister, Pierre Laval. Murder in Paris of C.'s first publisher, Robert Denoël. J.-P. Sartre, 'Portrait d'un anti-semite', an attack on C., suggesting he was in the pay of the Nazis.
1947	In hospital, then released, but not allowed to leave Denmark without official authorisation. Finishes second volume of *Guignol's Band*, starts writing *Féerie pour une autre fois*.	André Gide wins Nobel Prize for Literature.
1948	C. and Lucette move to house on the Baltic. Visits from French friends and sympathisers. His books start reappearing in France.	

1950	C's trial opens in Paris in his absence. Found guilty of collaboration and sentenced to a year's imprisonment, a fine of 50,000 francs, 'national degradation' and the confiscation of all his property.	Roger Nimier, *Le Hussard bleu*, anarchistic novel by C.'s most gifted young postwar admirer and friend.
1951	Amnestied and allowed to return to France. Settles in Meudon, in SW Paris, and resumes practising medicine.	
1952	All his books, except for the pamphlets, republished by the leading French publisher, Gallimard. First volume of *Féerie pour une autre fois* published, but generally ignored.	
1954	Second volume of *Féerie* appears, also *Entretiens avec le Professeur Y*, in which C. discusses his aims and methods as a writer.	Siege and surrender of Dien Bien Phu ends French campaigns and colonialism in Indo-China. Rising in Algiers against French rule launches Algerian war.
1956	The *Voyage* comes out as a mass paperback, and C. gives more and more interviews etc.	
1957	Publication of *D'Un château l'autre* (*Castle to Castle*), the first volume of a trilogy based on C's experiences in Germany in 1944–5.	
1958		End of Fourth Republic. De Gaulle returns to power.
1959	Five of C's unperformed scenarios for ballets published as a book.	
1960	Publication of *Nord* (*Nord*), second volume of the German trilogy.	
1961	At work on the final volume of the trilogy, *Rigodon*, published only in 1969. July 1, C. dies of a brain haemorrhage, aged sixty-seven. Buried in Meudon.	

Chapter 1

Introduction

Journey to the End of the Night is one of the great landmarks of modern writing, a work of vivid, caustic and eloquent misanthropy without its equal in French or any other literature. It set the tone very memorably, and prophetically, some sixty years ago for the age of now endemic pessimism about the potentialities for malice in human nature and about the future of our species. It expresses as no other book the condition of frustrated, secular humankind, whose lives know neither grace nor fulfilment but who have no beliefs of any sort to make them suppose things will ever be any better. The most that they can hope for is to endure, by finding distraction. Yet for all its sometimes vicious pessimism, the *Journey* has been for many of its millions of readers an enjoyable book, for in it Céline raises his negative feelings to the level of art, and makes it easy for us to admire the virtuosity of their expression. If he hoped to lower our spirits, by bringing us to share in his own gloomy philosophy of life, then he failed: such is the accomplishment − and I should add, the black humour − of his novel that its effect is the opposite. We unreservedly take to him as a writer despite his values.

From Destouches to Céline

Astoundingly, the *Journey* was a first book, and not of a fulltime writer but of a practising doctor. When it came out, in 1932, Céline was thirty-eight years old and working, under his real name of Destouches, at a municipal clinic in northern Paris. After the resonant publication of his novel, there could be no going back to the anonymity of Destouches, though he continued to practise medicine under that name until his death. He had also, in the 1920s, put it to his occasional medical writings: to the memoranda he drew up for the League of

Nations, for whose health services he worked for three quarrelsome years, to his journalism in the professional press, on public health questions such as sickness insurance and vaccination, and above all to the astonishing thesis which he wrote at the time when, as a mature student, he was qualifying as a doctor.

On this thesis we must pause, because in both its topic and its literary style it is emphatically a part of Céline's *œuvre* – indeed, it was published commercially four years after the *Journey*, following his success as a novelist. Its title is *The Life and Work of Semmelweis* and it is an angry, moralising account of the road to self-destruction of its subject, a Hungarian doctor of the mid-nineteenth century who was the first to recognise that puerperal fever was spread among women patients by the failure of obstetric staff to sterilise their hands; medical students might go straight from the dissecting table to the labour ward without washing. For all his efforts to convince his colleagues and the hospital authorities in Vienna of the truth of his discovery, Semmelweis was ignored and he became paranoiac at his rejection. Finally, in Céline's version of the story, he infects himself suicidally and dies. But university thesis or no, Céline's version is not scrupulously factual; he has twisted some of the known facts of Semmelweis's life and miserable death in order to draw his own bitter moral from them: that those who would be benefactors of the human race can expect only hostility and persecution in return. Céline's Semmelweis is the sacrificial victim of a society resistant to his idealism, he is a mythical, no longer a historical, let alone a medical figure. The distortions of history which Céline allows himself – they even run to swapping Semmelweis's first names round, from Ignaz-Philip to a gallicized Philippe-Ignace – were to be crucial to his practice of literature, in his thesis, in the *Journey*, in everything he wrote subsequently. He is an autobiographical writer who delights to misrepresent real events and characters, not least his own character, and the forms of his misrepresentation, where we are able to determine them, are a precious key to the nature of his temperament and intentions.

Dr Destouches had also written two plays, *Progrès* and *L'Église*, but had not been able to get them published. So in 1932 he was a complete stranger to the literary world, ambitious but untried. The *Journey* had been written in his evenings, after work, without much continuity; and it took him four years. Writing was the doctor's real life, but few people knew it. Once the manuscript was ready, it went to two publishers, to the great house of Gallimard, already France's best and most fashionable, and to the lesser house of Denoël and Steele. Gallimard havered, but Denoël did not; they accepted the book instantly, even though, the story goes, the manuscript came to them without the author's name and address on it, so that the sly, or forgetful, Dr Destouches had to be tracked down to his surgery in Clichy. The publication of so provocatively cynical a book was an event, causing outrage at one extreme, among the right-minded, and a corresponding delight at the other. And the fuss increased when this extraordinary first novel very nearly won the Prix Goncourt, far and away the most influential and profitable of French literary prizes. It was defeated only on the final vote of the jury, in dubious circumstances (common enough in the annual deliberations of the Goncourt jury) that later gave rise to litigation. Céline took quite easily to his celebrity and to his new double life, as humble doctor and as triumphant writer. He was angry at not having got the Goncourt, even if this was just the sort of hypocritical institution which, on the strength of what his novel had to say, he should have despised. But any such disappointment also gratified him, since it meant that he could continue to look on himself as a born outsider, too lucid in his perceptions of humankind ever to be received into its community.

On its first publication, then, the *Journey* caused much surprise, as a uniquely masterful first book by an unknown author, and equally much offence, as the vehicle of a repellently harsh philosophy of life, couched in a French never before thought fit to be put before respectable readers. Today, it is the offence it caused rather than the surprise that is of interest, because offensiveness has to do with the taste, the values and the formal expectations prevailing among readers at the time when the book appeared. Literary landmarks are very likely, even calculated, to upset their first audiences, so sharply do they break with precedent and with entrenched habits of reading. The *Journey* was not wholly unprecedented, for no book can be that, but what it instantly and dramatically did was to refocus tendencies in modern writing that had previously been only tentative and scattered, so reorientating the course of fiction in France away from seemly, essentially bourgeois subjects and milieux, and towards more vicious, low-life ones. As such, the *Journey* might seem simply like a return to the preoccupations of late-nineteenth-century naturalism, to the experiments of Maupassant or Emile Zola. But Céline thought naturalism a tame affair, half-hearted at best in its efforts to break with the conventions of polite literature. Six months after the *Journey* was published he gave the one public address of his life, in an act of homage supposedly to Zola. But Zola hardly came into it, as Céline expressed his own horror of the modern world, with its madness, its sadism and its universal 'death-instinct'. Zola in his day had been an optimist, able to look ahead in hope to some profound and saving amendment of the social and political scheme; Céline had no such hopes and would write accordingly, in an apocalyptic, hallucinatory mode explicitly removed from naturalism but better suited to the terminal degeneracy of the lives he saw all around him.

These remarks of Céline's relate to a vital aspect of his own writings. At no time did he aspire to be a realist, representing his society in such terms as to make that representation seem lifelike. On the contrary, he wanted it to appear other than lifelike, as the heightened product of its author's agitated vision. It was not our common world which Céline sought to represent, but his own uncommon one, and here is the divide between Destouches the doctor and Céline the writer. Céline's medical experience may have been useful to him once he had become an author, but he employs it metaphorically rather than literally, to support his vision of a contemporary society diseased in every respect, in body, in mind and in its institutions. His *œuvre* is less that of a doctor made unusually sensitive to the precariousness of physical existence by the experience of his practice than that of a prophet who believes that all the world bar himself is living on the surface of life, unaware of the omnipresence of death that undermines its solidity. The experience of Dr Destouches is not adequate to explain the morbid obsession of Louis-Ferdinand Céline.

From Céline to Bardamu

Three things were found offensive about the *Journey* on its first publication: the black, seemingly unrelieved cynicism of its central character, Bardamu; the subject-matter, much of it deemed obscene by the standards of the day; and the 'low', colloquial French in which it was written. This in fact was a calculatedly philistine novel, which brought a new note of grim humour and moral anarchy into French literature, as well as opening it up to registers of popular usage previously inadmissible there. These were three kinds of provocation offered by Céline in his own person, as a newcomer to literature who wanted at all costs to be identified as a trespasser, as the bearer of disturbing news about the world of which literature purported to be a depiction. The *Journey* is thus 'anti-literature', a ferocious example of a style of writing intended to unseat from within the decorous, tired conventions on which literature had hitherto been resting, by offering itself as literature of a new, brash and antagonistic kind.

Céline's overriding motive was to enter literature by force, and to bring to it a tone of voice for which there was no literary precedent, a disenchanted, resentful, 'popular' voice with not a grain of idealism to soften it. This, in the *Journey*, is the voice of Bardamu, the novel's mordant, egotistical narrator: the voice of Bardamu, not the voice of Céline the man, because the two are not the same. The attitudes of Bardamu are far from being those of the good Dr Destouches. It is true that, as the years passed, Céline took a more and more direct role as the narrator of his books, so that there is increasingly little scope for distinguishing between his social and his literary personae; he became, with practice, the prisoner of a character created first for literary effect, a real-life Bardamu. But in the *Journey* narrator and novelist are not yet one; this is more of an orthodox fiction than anything else that Céline wrote, and it makes obvious allowance for the conventions of the genre into which he had newly broken.

The novel has a story in it, and it ends in patent melodrama, with one − offstage − murder being followed by a second, this time on-stage. These are concessions to the requirements of fiction, as Céline conceived of them at the outset of his career, and the *Journey* would perhaps have been a still more effective book had the plot stopped short of actual murder. According to Bardamu, 'kill or be killed' is the rule men live by, but we read that adage figuratively, without needing to be convinced of its truth by having it put into practice. The *Journey* anyway *is* a novel, and not a tract, a picaresque novel in its form, in the course of which Bardamu travels extensively, through time as well as space. These travels have behind them the travels of Céline himself, in the sense that he too went to the places and passed through some of the experiences accorded to Bardamu. Céline was a conspicuously footloose person, and knew in his own life the oscillation between immobility and adventure so characteristic of the fortunes of his fictional hero. Bardamu is a picaresque hero in his movement about the world and in his lucidity towards it, because he travels for the purpose of revealing the secret and unlovely truth about human societies. The apparent variety of the settings in which he finds himself dissolves into a grim unity once this truth has been uncovered. There are four such settings in the novel, the First World War, colonial Africa, the industrialised United States, and the poor quarters of Paris; all are scenes of which Céline had direct experience, but in every case it is the departures from that experience − the novelist's known distortions − that tell us most about him. In the four sections which follow I will trace some of these wilful misrepresentations of fact and provide a brief historical context for them in the circumstances of Céline's life and times.

The war

Céline said repeatedly, to friends and to interviewers, that the First World War had been the one truly momentous and illuminating experience of his life, opening his eyes definitively and in an unforgettably cruel fashion to the stupid, internecine ways of men. By the late 1920s, when the *Journey* was being written, there was already talk in France of another European war being unavoidable, to settle the unfinished business of the first one, and Céline, the veteran of 1914, had reached the simple, if not at all general or popular, conviction that peace should be preserved at any cost, that there was no cause, no policy, no ideal, worth fighting or, more pertinently, worth dying for. To stay alive was itself the highest ideal, and an ideal naively destructive of all ideologies.

This was not at all the view that Céline had held in 1914. He was then twenty years old and an NCO in the cavalry, having joined the army as a volunteer two years before. He entered the war with the unthinking confidence and patriotism of the good soldier, able to write for example to his parents, on the point of leaving for the front: 'As for me, I shall do my duty to the very end and if by mischance I were not to return [. . .] be assured so as to lessen your pain that I die content, and thanking you from the bottom of my heart [. . .]' Within a few weeks of writing that letter, he had seen action in north-east France and was writing to his parents in less uplifting terms; he has seen much death and horror, and now realises that soldiers can tolerate such unnerving spectacles only because they are too exhausted to react to them. A transition was under way, though even the chastened Céline was very far from being a Bardamu. Bardamu is a gross anachronism, an ignoble character through whom Céline can project himself back into the killing-fields of Flanders from the vantage-point of the late 1920s, so as to demonstrate what he now regards, or affects to regard, as the one sane response to war. The objection to it now is basic: war kills people, and above all the wrong people, the young, who have years of life ahead of them. It kills them moreover for no adequate reason, merely making of them sacrifices in the service of what, in the *Journey,* is mocked as the 'religion of the flag'.

Céline's own war record in 1914 was brief but glorious; he was wounded in action, carrying despatches under fire, and awarded the Médaille Militaire; he was a minor hero of a campaign that was turning out very badly for the French army. Bardamu's behaviour on the field of action, on the contrary, is base and also bewildered. On being shot at, he has the age-old reaction of the civilian caught up in a military event he cannot understand: why are they shooting at me, I've not done them any harm? His egotism is complete, his one wish to avoid being killed. What is worse, and peculiarly Célinian, is that the threat to his person comes not only from the of-ficial enemy, the Germans, but also from his own side, which loses no opportunity of shooting French soldiers for cowar-dice. (This too is an anachronism, since in 1914 there were no such shootings in the French army. It is possible that there were some later, in 1916–17, when the warlike spirit of 1914 had long faded and local mutinies were endangering morale – but Céline is here exploiting rumour, not fact.) Céline's purpose in intruding this element of what amounts for him to civil war is to assimilate the conditions of Flanders more closely to those of society in general, which is seen as an inex-piable conflict between individuals. This assimilation is made stronger by the emphasis in the wartime passages of the *Journey* on the enmity between officers and men, and the class division it is built on, whereby the officers live off the fat of the land while the men are half-starved and sleep rough. Céline is doing much more here than truthfully recapturing his personal experience of war: he is imposing the grievous social divisions of peacetime on the real camaraderie in ex-tremis of the battlefield.

Bardamu's abject behaviour takes on a different colouring once we know of Céline's own bravery in 1914; Céline indeed is using his war record, the wound he got and the medal, to make his argument for an absolute pacifism seem the more compelling. He is trying through Bardamu to undo his own real-life heroism as it were, in a typical act of self-denigration.

For all his avowed cowardice Bardamu too wins a decoration, though the text does not tell us how. This is an asset to him during his convalescence, which covers some sixty pages of the novel and is an opportunity for Céline to bring out the terrible gap between the ordeal of the soldiers at the front and the ignorant jingoism of the civilians, either making merry at the rear or else literally cashing in on the disruptions of wartime. Here, again, is the distinction he loves to draw between those who know, and who suffer from knowing, and those who neither know nor suffer. Of the months of Céline's own convalescence we have little reliable evidence. He spent them being treated in hospital for the injury to his arm. What is striking about Bardamu as a war hero, however, is the falsity of the role he plays as such. He treats his medal as a stage-prop, showing it off at a Paris theatre on the day he receives it, and also as an erotic lure to attract Lola, one of the two girls with whom he has liaisons in these months. Later his unrecorded feat of arms, by now declared to be an 'invention', becomes the subject of an 'epic poem' which is recited on stage to much acclaim by an actress after whom the predatory Bardamu also lusts. Interestingly, the poem's author, a young man much too delicate to have been called to the colours – a homosexual, it turns out – is referred to as a 'barde' (a not very common term in French for a poet), which establishes a close link between him and the subject of his poem, the heroic Bard-amu. (The word *barde* is Celtic in origin, as Céline claimed his own family to be, so associating himself with a famously lyrical, imaginative verbal tradition.) This histrionic inflation of a presumably modest military exploit exemplifies one way of turning life into literature, by aggrandising it out of all recognition and at the same time expropriating it, since Bardamu is perfectly upstaged as an object of public attention by the recital itself. As an episode, it mirrors the very act on which Céline is here himself engaged, of making literature from his own life; but where the 'barde' aggrandises life, Céline belittles it; an opposite, less familiar and more devious process to which I shall have good cause to come back.

Africa

The second of the four major experiences that Céline makes use of in the *Journey* is his stay in French colonial Africa. He had been twice to Africa, first in 1916–17, and a second time in 1926, leading a health mission from the League of Nations. But it was his first, wartime visit which counted for most, undertaken when he was impressionable and was only a junior employee of a trading company, not, as in 1926, an international bureaucrat, travelling in some style. His stay, in French Cameroun, lasted ten months, even though he had signed on with the company for an engagement of two and a half years; but to the after-effects of his war wound there were added various disorders contracted locally, and he returned prematurely to France on grounds of health.

It was in West Africa that Céline seems to have begun to write, and the letters that he wrote home from there show at times a fluency, wit and idiosyncrasy remarkable in someone who had left school at fourteen. His aim in going to Cameroun was twofold, to get as far away from the European war as he could, and to earn some money, with a view to going on to the far more desirable continent of North America. Paradoxically, Cameroun was in 1916 a territory freshly won by French and British troops from the Germans, whose sovereignty over it had been confirmed after the Agadir incident and the consequent Franco-German agreement of 1911. When Céline arrived there, therefore, Cameroun was not an old French colony but a brand-new one, though there is no indication of this recent change of ownership in the events nor in the make-up of the local society as portrayed in the *Journey*.

The manner of Bardamu's arrival, in a territory now renamed as Bambola-Bragamance, is lurid compared with that of Céline. Céline sailed from Liverpool, on a ship called the *Accra* owned by the British and African Steam Navigation Company, as one, company records suggest, of only two passengers. Bardamu travels by a piratical shipping line called the Compagnie des Corsaires Réunis, on a vessel named the

Amiral Bragueton, and as one passenger among a hundred and twenty. His account of this voyage is one of the finest set-pieces of the novel, a brilliantly warped episode of paranoia to set alongside the tormented pleasure cruise of Evelyn Waugh's Gilbert Pinfold, when Pinfold, like Bardamu, imagines himself to be the butt of a quite irrational shipboard persecution. Waugh's novel, *The Ordeal of Gilbert Pinfold*, was based on an unsettling experience of real paranoia, Céline's was not: the passage of Bardamu to Africa is a miniaturised version of his passage through life as a whole, a voyage within the voyage so to speak, and as such a parable of the innate ferocity of our species − I shall have more to say about this episode in the section dealing with the theme of the voyage, on page 28.

For Céline the experience of Africa was positive: he found there space, to escape the too great proximity of other people, and he found independence of action. These were strong needs of his nature that so far in his life he had been obliged to suppress, first in the quite straitened milieu of his family, then in various jobs as a shop-boy, and not least in the army, where those protective of their independence cannot expect a good time. In Cameroun he achieved a sense of freedom and, so he assured his childhood girl-friend and correspondent, Simone Saintu, moments of pure happiness: 'I delight selfishly in the present minute − I think that is the one form of human happiness, the only one which doesn't let us down, the one we are really sure of, because it doesn't depend on anyone else.' Céline had no taste for nature (except for the sea) − for Bardamu, even the civilised greenery of the Bois de Boulogne is too much − but in its tropical forms nature had the virtue of excess and so answered to the major requirement of his imagination. As a correspondent, he gave the tropics their due; Bardamu, however, will have none of it, he is disgusted by 'the poetry of the Tropics' and gladly leaves them to their natural denizens, the 'mosquitoes and the panthers'.

Africa for Bardamu is an irredeemably negative place, of an atrocious and, for many white people, fatal climate and of a way of life founded on corruption, sadism, concupiscence and deceit. Far from fostering independence, colonial society is closed and hierarchical, with the Governor at its head, and beneath him descending classes of traders, administrators, soldiers and natives. Each class is at war with the others, and within the classes each individual is out to exploit every other. Bardamu recognises two kinds of colonialism, one which is straightforwardly brutal, and chastises the natives in order to keep them in line socially and economically; the other, more modern, affects to trade with rather than to tyrannise them, but it is equally exploitative. Bardamu, the supreme realist, favours the first kind because it is overt in its racism and makes no pretence to humanity; Céline, the novelist, seizes gratefully on the second, apparently more benevolent kind, in order to unmask the hypocrisy on which he claims that it depends. What is not represented in the novel is the humanity which he seems to have displayed himself, as a temporary resident in West Africa.

In the *Journey* Blacks form the necessary underclass of Bambola-Bragamance, for racially the colony is a second war zone, divided into two as Flanders had been, with the natives now as the cannon fodder, ready to be sacrificed for the gratification and profit of their superiors, the officer-class colonists. The Blacks' chief characteristic is passivity; they are whipped, swindled, despised, but they show no signs of wishing to revolt against their situation. Rather, they connive in their fate and, given the chance, ape the avaricious mores of the whites: when Bardamu is finally carried in a high fever out of the forest by some of the local people, he asks himself why they should be helping him in this way, why people he claims to be cannibals should be rescuing him, when they might be eating him. He is given the answer once he has reached the coast and finds himself on a galley: they have sold him into slavery. In Cameroun, Céline showed a real and practical sympathy for black people; in his novel, they differ from the whites only in their opportunities, not at all in their actions, which are fully as despicable.

Céline in fact discovered both his vocations during his time in Africa, beginning there first to write and then, however amateurishly, to practise medicine. Faced with the upsetting evidence of endemic and untreated disease among the native population, he sent home to his father in Paris for elementary medical supplies – needles, syringes, basic chemicals. Such medical knowledge as he then had can only have been got from books or from conversation with doctors and nurses. But in his letters to Simone Saintu he could present himself as a potential benefactor of the indigenous population, a would-be Semmelweis: '[. . .] I am attempting to do some good, I run a pharmacy, I look after as many blacks as possible, though I'm not at all convinced of their usefulness.' This closing qualification is equivocal: is Céline anxious to show that he at least is no mere utilitarian, caring for the Blacks only in order to make them more productive, or is he simply associating himself with the white suprematist view of them? In print, later in his life, Céline was unquestionably a racist, predicting dire consequences of miscegenation between Aryan whites and other skin-colours, but his record as a practising doctor was always impeccable, he would treat anybody, the deprived classes especially. The two incompatible sides of him are already on display in this letter from 1916.

The West Africa of the *Journey* is a site of disease and bodily degradation far worse than any reality, for in describing it Céline has literally turned up the heat, so that previously solid human organisms are threatened constantly by an equatorial melt-down. This is a process of liquefaction that starts indeed on the boat, once 'past Portugal', when the passengers of the *Amiral Bragueton* start to dissolve and to be revealed in all their true physical and moral infirmity. The effect of tropical heat is quite simply to bring out the *truth* about them, which is that they are perishable bodies, whose inexorable corruption will be accelerated in such extremes of climate. Bambola-Bragamance is thus a territory inhabited almost entirely by the chronically sick, and the novelist dwells in delight on the variety and persistence of the various forms of local malady. Here some of what Céline will have learnt of the types and incidence of tropical diseases as a League of Nations tourist in

1926 comes into play. At the time of his own stay Bardamu already has some medical knowledge, having begun but then broken off his studies, and the effect of that is to isolate him in this profoundly unhealthy community, since he trusts in his rational abstemiousness, as a man who does not drink or smoke ('Are you a pederast?' asks the suspicious manager of his company), to save him from the organic ruin affecting everyone else.

But he does not use his medical knowledge to help others. Far from sensing in himself any vocation to be a doctor, he senses an opposite vocation, to be a patient. In the novel the hospital of Fort-Togo, the colony's capital, is given a perverse role to play. Bardamu looks on it as a refuge, a blessed spot, 'an earthly paradise' almost, not because it treats the sick but because it is an asylum from the viciousness of local life; in the hospital, reflects Bardamu, a man is sheltered from 'the men outside, the bosses', it offers him a respite of freedom from the condition of servitude in which he must otherwise spend his time. His vocation of patient presents an exact and interesting reversal of the therapeutic vocation aroused in Céline himself during his short time in Cameroun.

The United States

In his flight from Africa the ailing Bardamu travels directly to New York the hard way, as an oarsman on a slave galley, a fantastic transit to match his arrival aboard the *Amiral Bragueton*, and a jocular reference on Céline's part to the notorious Middle Passage across the Atlantic, which was for long the principal conduit by which West African Negroes were carried to North America and sold into labour there (Bardamu of course has been sold into labour *by* Blacks). In terms of Céline's own life this galley-trip subsumes the long and highly formative period between his return to France from Cameroun in 1917 and his first visit to North America eight years later. In this time he had qualified as a doctor, had married, and soon enough separated from, the daughter of his professor in Rennes, and had been taken on by the public hygiene section of the League of Nations in Geneva. In 1925 the League sent him to the United States for three months, as guide to a party of South American doctors (English he had learnt quite thoroughly, first at two schools in Kent, and then in the year spent in London in 1915–16, working at the French consulate). This was a formal tour, repetitive and mainly a tedious round of visits to American public health facilities. But if it was tedious it was performed in comfort, and it introduced Céline to features of American life that a normal tourist would not have seen.

The United States had long been in his mind as a country to go to; in his letters from Africa he is already speaking of it as the most attractive of possible destinations. His first reaction to New York when eventually he got there was given in a short letter to his superiors in Geneva: 'Whatever I see is like nothing else, it's mad, like the war', a snap judgment of which the pages of the novel set in the United States are an elaboration. In this novel, as we have begun to see, all the settings are like the war, since war is merely peace conducted by more openly lethal means. In important respects, however, the United States is the most congenial of the four places in which Bardamu finds himself, with something at least to commend it. It is not a friendly place, least of all for a foreigner without the money by which to ingratiate himself with dollar-worshipping Americans, and Bardamu reflects Céline's own sense of being diminished and humiliated there, as a nobody ill at ease in a progressive society. There are also grotesqueries in its portrayal, such as the extraordinary description of an open-plan men's lavatory underneath the shopping streets of Manhattan, which is a faecal reminder that one of the writers whom Céline most admired was Rabelais – as well as one more evidence of his obsession with liquefaction.

Bardamu's experience in America, unlike Céline's own, is materially uncomfortable. He is desperate for money almost from the moment he lands there, and thus able to feel at one with the large local population of *miteux* or the down-at-heel. But the country has two things to offer him, both of which were central to its attraction for Céline also: the cinema and

American women. Céline had a great liking for the cinema, and on much the same grounds as the young Sartre (early on a film-fan, as readers of his autobiographical *Les Mots* will remember), to wit that it was a 'popular' and not a bourgeois entertainment. The cinema was cheap, it was as yet 'low' and not 'high' art, and to enjoy it was to associate yourself with 'the people'. But Céline's love of it went deeper, because as a writer he felt a deep kinship of purpose with it. The cinema trades the most blatantly and effectively of all media in fantasy, and by the 1920s was already bringing blissful distraction into otherwise bleak and tedious lives which sorely needed it. It was a medium both available to the working class and essentially urban, and as a 'dream factory' Céline looked on it as a genuine agency of social therapy, a provider of placebos for the masses. In New York Bardamu finds comfort in the cinema, which is a refuge for him from loneliness and from the hostility of the streets, just as the hospital had been in Fort-Gono.

As for American women, Céline idealised them, especially during the years when he was writing the *Journey*, when his regular companion was the American dancer Elizabeth Craig, whom he had first met in Geneva and who went with him back to Paris. A majority of the recorded liaisons of his life were with ballet dancers, whom he admired for their athleticism and for the exemplary, as if reassuring, firmness of their bodies. For some reason he believed that the United States was a country ahead of all others in the production of such healthy and desirable bodies, a view of it which is accentuated in the novel. There, Bardamu first encounters this transatlantic ideal, when, as a wounded soldier, convalescing amidst the fleshpots of Paris, he meets 'Lola from America', a volunteer nurse who has come to help 'save France'. The hardened Bardamu feels unwontedly kindly towards her naivety and her optimism, expressive as they are of her native country, to which he is at once drawn as a potential sexual utopia. And on his arrival in New York an unspecified number of years later the women are indeed there, as promised: first the 'glorious', tennis-playing fifteen year-old daughter of the comically named Major Mischief on Ellis Island, and then, in the hitherto sad streets of Manhattan, around midday, 'a sudden avalanche of absolutely beautiful women'. The wartime example of Lola has not deceived him, Bardamu reflects, even though Lola herself, when met with again, is a wrinkled, malign disappointment, a source of dollars but no longer of simple carnal pleasure. But there is better, and younger, than Lola: in Detroit there is Molly, the prostitute who brings Bardamu solace from his dehumanising work in the car factory. Molly stands out quite garishly in the novel for being, as fictional prostitutes so frequently have been, golden-hearted; but she is American and therefore, for Céline, a figure to be dreamt of, a seductive figment.

As a League of Nations missionary he presumably had little opportunity to realise his erotic imaginings in the United States. His concern was with public health, and with the American practice of it. Among the visits that the delegation made were two, both very brief, to major industrial centres, in order to learn how large employers in America cared for the health of their employees. In the later 1920s this was a topical question in France, where many thought that there should now be started a state scheme of sickness insurance. With his party Céline went to the Ford Motor Company's celebrated factory in Detroit and to Westinghouse in Pittsburgh, visits that were to influence him greatly and to be a point of reference in his writings. The report which he wrote for his superiors in Geneva on the lessons he claimed could be learnt from the manner in which Ford looked after the welfare of its workforce makes strange but significant reading.

By the mid-1920s Ford in Detroit was a byword, in western Europe as in North America, as the world's first great example of mass-production, of an assembly line geared to the manufacture in unprecedented numbers of what, by the standards of the time, were cheap cars. What most struck Céline about this model factory, by his own account, was its apparent open-door policy, whereby it would take on anybody at all to work there, whatever the state of their health. In the novel Bardamu, having come to Detroit and being in need of money, is taken on after only the most superficial of medical examinations, despite the disabilities he suffers from; the examining doctors do not fail to spot them, they simply ignore them. Such an employment policy might sound generous, even enlightened, and something like it had indeed been in force at Ford in the years immediately following the end of the 1914–18 war. By the time of Céline's visit to Detroit, however, the policy of the company had grown more stringent. But even in his official report to the League of Nations, he exaggerates greatly Ford's indifference to the physical condition of its prospective employees, claiming for example that a single doctor at the factory might complete up to 350 medicals in one day, so perfunctory were they. Such a hyperbolic account of Ford's methods belongs in the novel, and not where it eventually finished up, in the very serious archives in Geneva. And Céline's credibility hardly improves as he goes on to describe the Ford factory as a 'clinical museum', filled almost entirely with the physically incapable (shades, we would say, of Bambola-Bragamance).

What was the purpose of falsifications of this order, included as they were in an official report? They enabled Céline to reach a large and tendentious conclusion as to the nature of industrial society. The point which he repeatedly makes in his report is that with the new degree of mechanisation which has been reached at Ford, human operatives on the assembly-line no longer need to be either skilled or healthy. They are interchangeable in their functions, and so unspecific is their work that the absence of particular individuals is of no account – Céline claims even to have been told by a doctor in Detroit that chimpanzees would be equally as effective in the plant as men (a remark made also to Bardamu in the novel). The industrial philosophy behind such an organisation of work was known as Taylorism, and it was giving rise in those years to much argument and alarm, so inhumane did it seem. Taylorism had not yet come to France, in the 1920s an industrially backward country, but the prospect of it was deeply disagreeable, especially to someone like Céline, nostalgic as he often expressed himself to be for the individualistic artisanal world of the nineteenth century, before Progress became the great, heartless engine of societies.

Logically, therefore, his description of the Ford factory and its employment policies, both in his League of Nations report and as transposed in the *Journey*, ought to be thoroughly negative, as of a perfectly undesirable place of work. In the novel the car factory is indeed, and predictably, a hellish place, full of an intolerable level of noise which reduces those who work all day in it to vacuous ciphers. Yet in his medical writings, both published and unpublished, Céline presents a markedly different view of the Ford philosophy, as some sort of model for the future. This seems radically inconsistent. But the fact is that like a majority of French doctors, and despite his sympathies for the *miteux*, Céline was not in favour of a state insurance scheme, and offers Ford's system as a reasonable alternative to it. The state has no need to concern itself with the health of the working population, and above all with those members of it incapacitated from work, if employers can be got to do so instead. But there is a typical extremism in his position: if the nature of work changes, as it has done at Ford, so that the incapacitated become employable, then the work-place becomes the focus of any sound policy of social hygiene and it is there that patients should, if they need it, be treated. Subsequently, Céline went beyond even this ruthless vision of a factory-centred medicine, to support the formation of 'a vast medical and sanitary police force, which would reach out not only to the home of the person insured, but above all to the places where he works [. . .]'. This sounds, and was surely meant to sound, chilling; but almost lost to view in it is a humane premise, of which Céline made much, that care of the sick would be much advanced if the carers had more firsthand acquaintance with the often noxious environments in which people lived and worked. This laudable argument makes an excellent bridge to the next section, which relates Bardamu's experiences as a GP in Paris to that of Céline.

Paris

Whatever sympathy Céline may originally have felt for the purposes and programmes of the League of Nations, by 1927 it had evaporated. He no longer liked his employers, and his employers had become intolerant of him, as a sardonic individualist not to be accommodated in a bureaucracy. In one of the two plays which he wrote at this time, *L'Eglise*, there is much frankly ponderous satire of the League's ways, of the avarice of its medical specialists, of its love of unproductive discussion, of its mountainous paperwork. There is anti-semitism also, the pricipal culprits for the organisation's failings being shown as a group of conspiratorial Jews. Céline's superior, and his one supporter in Geneva was himself Jewish, but he was paid out in *L'Eglise* by appearing there in the unlovely character of Yudenzweck, the coldly scheming 'director of the Service of Compromises' (this same Jewish target, Ludwig Rajchman, was later attacked far more unpleasantly by Céline, in *Bagatelles pour un massacre*).

In 1927, he left Geneva and the League of Nations 'on sick leave', six months before his three-year contract was up, and in November of that year set up as a general practitioner in Paris, in the shabby northern suburb of Clichy. He was in need of money, having left spectacular debts behind him in Geneva, but his private practice did not provide very much of it. He had, however, found the setting for the second half of the *Journey*, in which Bardamu, now fully qualified as a doctor, puts up his brass plate in 'his sort' of suburb, La Garenne-Rancy. This is a made-up name, richly expressive as all Céline's made-up names are: *la garenne* is both the French for a rabbit warren and also the name of a real suburb of Paris, adjacent to that outlying quarter of the city in which he had himself been born, Courbevoie (now almost absorbed into the grandiose new financial and high-rise office quarter of La Défense; how Céline would have thundered against that!), while Rancy, or *ranci*, is our 'rancid' and intended to be descriptive of life as lived in this populous and unfavoured warren. (A further determinant of this place-name was perhaps the Cirque Rancy,

a travelling circus famous in the last century; circuses are raf-
fish, nomadic entertainments of a kind Céline admired. There
is also an eastern suburb of Paris called Le Raincy).

Céline plays obvious games with the real topography of Paris
in the novel, as when he first indicates that the northern quarter
of La Garenne-Rancy is to be reached by way of the Porte
Brancion, which is in fact on the opposite, southern side of
Paris. But he gives accurate indications too, to identify Rancy
with the real quarter of Clichy, and sufficient references to the
Place Clichy, a little to the north of the Gare St. Lazare and
a focal point of Montmartre, to make this the epicentre of
Bardamu's career in Paris, as it was long that of Céline himself.
He took gladly on his return from Switzerland to the rough,
vaguely dangerous life of Montmartre, a quarter of the city
which had changed by 1930 from being the home of more or
less respectable avant-garde artists to being the principal haunt
of Parisian low-life. There are plentiful echoes of Montmartre's convivial underworld in the novel, in the presence
there of the pimp Pomone, of the local prostitutes, of the
English dance troupe at the Tarapout cinema (a name, this
time, modelled phonetically on the common Paramount).

Céline's attempt to run a medical practice on his own was
a failure; he was incapable either of looking the part or of
behaving with the decorum asked for from 'the doctor', and
he regularly treated his poorest patients for nothing. He took
a part-time job as publicist for a pharmaceutical laboratory
and early in 1929 a second part-time job, in the newly opened
municipal clinic of Clichy, where he was on duty only for an
hour and a half a day, so leaving him time free for his writing. But
even if he was far from prosperous, he was still a professional
man and his fortunes never fell as low as those of Bardamu, who
is constantly on the point of starvation and finds it impossible to
get money from his grudging patients. Céline himself chose to
practice in a working-class suburb not out of saintliness so much
as out of a desire to mark himself off from the bourgeois medical
establishment which he thought knew nothing of the wretched
conditions in which many Parisians lived. What is more, he had
just spent two and a half years in the abstract world of the League
of Nations, where actual bodily suffering had been comfortably

disguised as tables of comparative statistics. Clichy was thus reality, an exposure to life as it is and at the same time a rebuke to a medical profession disinclined to face up to such challenging truths. But Bardamu goes a great deal further than Céline did in dissociating himself, or being forcibly dissociated by his circumstances, from the bourgeois milieu of the orthodox doctor. There was it so happens a superfluity of doctors competing for patients in Paris in the late Twenties and early Thirties, and Céline's own practice may have languished accordingly; but no real doctor was ever so beset by poverty or by unsuccess as his fictional locum.

As a character Bardamu predates the *Journey*, he is the central figure also of *L'Eglise*, the final two acts of which are likewise set in a Paris suburb. Here Bardamu is the local doctor recommended for being 'cheap' — he has no surgery but works instead by appointment out of a bar, which is to carry Céline's belief in environmental medicine to pleasant extremes. The earlier Bardamu's medical philosophy is simple and self-defeating, and is summed up in his dictum, 'You don't need anyone else, to get better.' Such an outlook calls the very practice of medicine into question, since if it can not cure, what then is it for? The answer, for Bardamu, is that it has a social function, but only *in extremis*. Unlike other doctors who, he claims, abandon their patients in their death agony, vexed by their own scientific failure to find a cure, he stays and brings a last, needed relief to the dying: 'That's the moment when you're useful, y'know. It's for dying that you need someone.' This deliberately unprofessional philosophy is found again in the Bardamu of the novel, who is invariably fatalistic as to the course of the illness or conditions he is called upon to treat. Brutally fatalistic on occasions: just as in *L'Eglise* there is a crippled girl, in love with Bardamu, to whom he will offer no comfort as to the possible alleviation of her disability, so in the *Journey* he is equally sadistic when he tells Lola that there is no cure for her mother's liver cancer (at this point in the book he is not even supposed to be a qualified doctor). Bardamu is in fact a voyeur of sickness, convinced that it is endemic in the human condition and unresponsive to the therapeutic programmes of medical science. In *L'Eglise* he explains that he has 'got over' science, having grasped that the desire to understand on which science as an institution rests is merely one more evidence of fear, that we would better to be as animals are, and accept the sudden or the gradual impairment of our bodies.

Céline's own medical philosophy was not, needless to say, of the same bleak kind as Bardamu's. He had begun in medicine, as a layman in West Africa, with a practical desire to provide simple treatment for the chronically afflicted natives of the territory and he preserved some concern throughout his life for the positive virtues, the scientific virtues even, of medical intervention. But he was never a strong believer in its effectiveness; medicine had no cure for the supreme affliction, of death, nor for the unaesthetic degeneration of the human body from its youthful glory into the infirmity of old age. In *L'Eglise* Bardamu gives an ugly and remarkable answer when he is asked why he first decided to study medicine: 'Above all out of a fear of other men [. . .] There! I'd rather have to deal with the ones who are sick. The ones who are healthy are so vicious, so stupid [. . .]' It is as if sickness brought a social and a moral improvement to human character, as a condition which makes us less perniciously competitive with one another.

The evidence of friends and associates, however, is that Céline was genuinely angry and distressed by the evidence of ill-health which he found all around him in the grime of Clichy. A medical colleague recalled him being 'weighed down by everything he saw in Clichy, by the working-class poverty he met with daily and by the tuberculosis whose ravages he discovered every day'. In the most trenchant and important of his medical papers, an unpublished 'memorandum' of 1932 (the same year as the *Journey* was published), he attacked public health specialists for their 'stupidity', for their 'almost total ignorance of the social reality', and looked forward to the 'spiritual revolution' that would come about when they finally discovered 'the world whose sanitary conditions they are in fact responsible for improving'. Here is the explanation of what the medically impotent Bardamu is doing in Rancy, and of his own fallen condition there: he is a witness to the unhealthy conditions in which people are obliged or else choose to live, and is no longer insulated from them by money. Céline's ideal was a social medicine without the medication as it were, and the clinical experiences of Bardamu in the *Journey* have in consequence little to do with the customary business of diagnosis or treatment, but everything to do with the harmfulness of the environment and the public health scourges that it secretes. There is more than merely squalor in the novel's descriptions of Parisian slum living:

Backyards, they're the dungeons of terrace houses. I had lots of time to myself to look at mine, my backyard, and especially to hear it.
    That's where the calls and shouts from the twenty houses round about come cascading, crashing, bouncing down, from the despairing pet birds of the concierges even, mouldering away in their cages and cheeping after a springtime they won't ever see again, next to the lavatories, that are all grouped together there, in the shadows at the end, with their doors always smashed and hanging off. A hundred drunkards, men and women, inhabit this brickwork and stuff the echoes with their boastful quarrelling, with a flood of doubtful swearwords, on Saturdays after lunch in particular. That's the moment when family life gets intense. They yell defiance at each other and they're plastered out of their minds, dad, look at him, he's wielding the chair like an axe and mum the log from the fire like a sabre! The weak had better watch out! It's the young one that cops it. Whatever can't defend itself and answer back is knocked flat against the wall, children, dogs or cats. After the third glass of wine, of black wine, the cheapest, it's the dog that starts to suffer, a big heel comes down on its paw. That'll teach it to be hungry at the same time as the humans [. . .]   (P 265–6 M 238–9)

There is no mistaking this nightmarish picture of life in Clichy for some reality as experienced by Céline. Its abjectness is grossly heightened partly in order to demonstrate his hatred of the intimacies of family life, with its victimisation of the defenceless, of the children and the household animals, but partly also to stress the impoverished milieu in which disease is inescapable: alcoholism brought on more rapidly by bad wine, tuberculosis made worse by inadequate nutrition, dysentery associated with poor sanitation, and so on. The descriptions of Rancy in the novel are a denunciation of the living conditions of many proletarians in Paris, because Céline recognised that the poor suffer a higher incidence of disease and death simply through not having the money to lead more salubrious lives.

Bardamu has one other medical experience in Paris in common with Céline, when he goes in search of scientific help from the Institut Bioduret Joseph, a research establishment from which, as it is portrayed in the novel, no good can ever have come, so futile are its activities. Céline himself had, during his medical training, worked briefly at the most celebrated of such establishments in Paris, the Institut Pasteur. The identification between the fictive institute and the real one was readily made by those who knew the Institut Pasteur, even though Céline has moved it diametrically across Paris, from the south-west quarter of the city to the north-east (on his return from the Institut, Bardamu reverts to an itinerary which replaces it in its rightful quarter). The Institut Bioduret is no temple of science. At eleven o'clock in the morning, when Bardamu gets there, it is deserted, full of a sinister jumble of things but no people: 'There was no one to be found as yet in the laboratories, scientists any more than public, nothing but objects tumbled in complete disorder, the eviscerated corpses of small animals, dog-ends, chipped gas jets, cages and jars with mice busy suffocating inside, retorts, bladders lying littered, broken stools, books and dust, and the prevailing smell, of everlasting dog-ends and the urinal' (P 279 M 249). Bardamu has come to this unpropitious centre, which seems to specialise more in death than the preservation of life, because he is perplexed by a case, of a boy whom he believes to have typhoid, and at the Institut is a famous specialist in the etiology of that disease. But the visit, naturally, is of no help to Bardamu; his young patient dies. Medical science, as conducted by the malicious and doubtfully sane research-workers on display at the Institut, has nothing to offer the victims of diseases that are socially determined.

Bardamu's final medical experience is as an assistant at the mental home run by the formidable Baryton, his career thus at the last departing from any such precedent in Céline's own. Céline had been in hospitals, as a convalescent in 1915 and during his medical training, and had perhaps worked at his father-in-law's small private clinic in Rennes ('La Sagesse' or 'Wisdom' was its name, which has its ironies if the clinic contained mental patients). But Baryton's asylum is, as we would expect, *sui generis*. It is located in another imaginary site, Vigny-sur-Seine, somewhere on the fringes of Paris. Vigny is remarkable for being in a state of transition, for being 'a village mutating into a suburb'. This was a process of urbanisation that Céline deplored, even though, with his resolutely town-bred tastes and indifference towards nature, he makes an incongruous defender of the countryside. But urbanisation is Progress, and that he was against, in all its forms. In Vigny-sur-Seine Progress means a new pretentiousness among the bourgeoisie and above all the loss of a past, of certain traditions, seen necessarily as better than what has replaced them:

It is losing a garden a month. Where you come in the posters are all the colours of the Ballet Russe. The town clerk's daughter knows how to mix cocktails. Only the tram's set on becoming historical, it'll need a revolution for that to go. People are worried, the children no longer have the same accent as their parents. They're embarrassed almost when they realise they're still in the Seine and Oise [i.e. in the administrative *département* of the S.-et-O.]. A miracle's happening. The last set of garden bowls vanished when Laval came to office and since the holidays the charwomen have put their price up by twenty centimes an hour [. . .]　　　　(P 422 M 368)

This satirical account of creeping suburbanisation might be dated by the reference to Pierre Laval, who became prime minister in France early in 1931. But Céline is mocking the progressive urges of the century as a whole, urges against which he grew shriller and shriller as time went by, in his detestation of modernity. The psychiatrist Baryton shares some of this detestation, though he is also modern or grasping enough to regret not having earlier bought more land around Vigny which he could now sell at a great profit for building plots. Left to himself, he would not have troubled to bring up to date his methods of treatment of his patients, given that no treatment at all will cure them, but he has had to experiment with therapeutic novelties because his clientèle expects it of him. This clientèle is not the patients themselves but the 'families' — Céline's *bête noire* once again — who have paid to put them away in his asylum. In an unforgettably florid and apocalyptic speech to Bardamu, Baryton dissociates himself from the modernists in his profession, and rants against the apostles of Progress, expressing the conviction, which was also that of Céline, that life began to go downhill in France in 1900, the year of the great Paris Exhibition.

Baryton is an ambiguous figure in the novel: he is himself decidedly unbalanced while declaring that it is the loss of balance which has destroyed psychiatry. He is, as his name indicates, a 'voice', and the reactionary opinions to which he gives vent are, by Céline's lights, admirable. The wilder he becomes in speech, the more uncomfortably he reminds one of the later Céline, anathematising all and sundry in the name of an imaginary past. Some of Baryton's shafts are implicitly directed at the Freudians, whose 'foreign' doctrines have introduced into pyschiatry a belief in the curative virtues of self-expression, or the oral expulsion of what has been repressed. Baryton finds this futile and disgusting. Céline, however, did not. He was no Freudian, but he could quote the best-known ideas of Freud and was an opportunist: he seized on the notion of a universal 'death-wish' because it consorted so well with his own dark philosophy of human instincts. Baryton, moreover, goes against his own avowed principles in disclosing opinions that his professional position would normally force him to keep to himself. Once he has spoken he is free, and after thirty years he can set irresponsibly off on his travels to nowhere, leaving his role at the asylum to the suddenly captive Bardamu. The two have changed places. But it is important for the novel that its hero should end where he began, in Paris; his journey has been circular because it was, necessarily, 'all in the mind'.

Chapter 2

Themes

The six themes analysed in this chapter are not the only ones which could be picked out from the *Journey*, nor those that other readers of the novel might pick out. But they serve here as especially productive headings under which to bring order, semantically, to a not always coherent text.

The voyage

Many of the stories which are told, in literature as also in life, have a voyage or journey for their organising theme: as a narrative thread it is as old as the *Odyssey*. In one sense, all narratives recount a 'voyage' inasmuch as they detail the passage from an initial state of affairs into another − usually happier, sometimes unhappier, but necessarily different − one. The voyage then becomes a metaphor for the displacement inseparable from the progress of a story. But here I shall stick to the voyage as a literal or explicit motif of fiction, as it is in the present case. Céline's hero (or else his anti-hero) is a voyager, he has a wanderlust, not because he is keen to see other places but because he is desperate to get away from wherever he finds himself. He cannot bear to be stationary for long. But Bardamu's travels amount to a parody of the literary genre to which they belong. The fictional voyager expects to be improved or gratified by the places he travels to, but with Bardamu this is absolutely not so. The places he travels to are as wretched as those he has come from; the effect of his mobility is to stop up the promising avenues of escape from a life which he finds unliveable.

Yet there is also a positive side to his voyaging, because it sets him up as a narrator. Bardamu remains the archetypal voyager: he is the privileged person who has been to some other place, who has *seen*, and who has now returned to tell those who have not been there what it is like. The account of his travels, however negative, will be our own welcome and vicarious distraction. The traveller's tale is of course essentially colloquial, it is a spoken form of narrative, ideal for someone as graphic and as versatile in his powers of narration as Bardamu. Céline was fond of reminding people that his family was Breton, i.e. Celtic, and that Celts above all can tell seductive stories; Bardamu, with his overtly bardic name, does just that. Late in the novel, when he is taken on by Baryton to work at the asylum, he leads his employer's mind away from the worries of his profession by recounting his travels over dinner. Baryton is hooked: 'Once we've heard you, we don't need to go and see these countries any more, you tell about them so well, Ferdinand!' (P 417 M 364). Which is just what the voyager, the supreme story-teller, wants to hear; Bardamu is a success, and in his pleasure grows unconcerned about the veracity of what he recounts.

Journey to the End of the Night is an account of a single moral voyage, as embodied in the French title (the English translators of the novel would have done well to keep it as 'voyage', and not diminished an old and honourable literary motif by turning it into the more everyday 'journey'), which itself contains a series of geographical voyages, or physical displacements about the map on the part of Bardamu. The plot of the novel is elementary, divided as it is into four more or less self-contained parts, set in different places; but at the same time this brokenness enhances the continuity afforded to the book by the consistently egregious Bardamu in his first-person narration. His tone of voice alone, and the cynical attitudes he expresses towards the events and characters he meets with, give the story a sufficient integrity, ensuring that here it is the qualities of the voyager and not the exoticism of his voyage which keeps us listening.

There are two strong reasons why Bardamu should travel in the literal sense, from place to place, one having to do with the novel's relation to the contemporary world, the other with his (or else perhaps the novelist's own) psychology. It would not have done for Céline to have set the action of the *Journey* exclusively in Paris, or even in France, when it was his wish to use his fiction to demonstrate a universal truth about humanity, that it lives everywhere by the fearsome law of 'Kill or be Killed'. The opening section of the novel, in which the subject-matter is a real war, inaugurates what becomes a se-quence of battle reports, from colonial Africa, from the in-dustrial United States, and finally from metropolitan Paris. Bardamu's mobility enables him to assimilate these variously punitive experiences one to the other, as necessary elements in his moral education, and in this respect one might typify him as a picaresque hero, set loose in the world the better to incorporate as much of it as is plausible into his pessimistic schema.

There is also a psychological side to the voyaging theme, however. Bardamu travels not simply to broaden the scope of the story but because temperamentally he must, for he can never be satisfied with the place where he is. He has the escapist's conception of travel so familiar to us from reading the great nineteenth-century Romantics: the 'voyage' is the one form of compensation open to those disgusted by any fix-ity of life, the best answer to modern *ennui*. Bardamu's restlessness is that well attested to in Céline himself, a refusal to stay put which can also turn into fury against all the many people for whom stability in life is a comfort and an ideal.

To travel for Bardamu is to seek release, and this can be true even of 'voyages' which are themselves both slight and hazardous. As a soldier he is entrusted by his local com-mander with what he calls by the not very warlike term of 'a delicate mission'. He is to get a horse and ride under cover of darkness to a town fourteen kilometres away, to settle the uncertain question of whether or not the enemy has taken it. This act of reconnaissance is a more complex and suggestive episode than some mere slice of battlefield life, recovered by Céline from memory. In the first place, the town Bardamu has to ride to has the name of Noirceur-sur-la-Lys, or literally translated, Blackness-on-the-Lily, which is not somewhere to be found on the maps of Picardy even if the Lys is a real river there and was indeed a part of the battle zone in 1914. But to this authentic toponym Céline has added the symbolism of his Noirceur, the significance of which I will come back to. Bardamu, who has by now learnt the vital lesson from his experience of war, that the sensible thing to be is a coward, because cowards may survive while brave men get slaughtered, undertakes the 'mission readily enough, even though logic dictates that he should not, given that it will be risky. But he accepts it because it is a 'voyage': 'It was a long time since I'd been alone. I suddenly seemed to be setting off on a voyage. But my deliverance was fictitious' (P 36 M 38). The odd wording of this reflection harks back to the exordium of the novel, which goes, in part: 'Voyaging's very useful, it sets the imagination working. All the rest's just disappointment and fatigue. Our own voyage is wholly imaginary. That's its strength' (P 5 M 7). The triple equation here, between voyaging, imagining and working is crucial. To imagine is to voyage in the mind, and for the imaginer who is also a writer, to imagine is to work: the imaginary voyage offers the fulfilment that a real one will very likely not offer (the etymological tie between English *travel* and French *travail* is worth reflecting on in this regard).

Bardamu's brief 'voyage', to Noirceur-sur-la-Lys, is very instructive for him; in the course of it he meets with evidence of cruelty to children, a minor but potent and recurrent theme of the novel, with the vacuous posturings of patriotic officialdom in the person of the despicable mayor of Noirceur, and above all with the strange figure of Robinson, his alter ego in the novel who shows up again and again in the course of it. (Robinson's function as a character I leave until the next section of this chapter; but his name, deriving from Defoe's Robinson Crusoe, connects all too plainly with the theme of the imaginary voyage as well as with the associated theme, just now broached by Bardamu, of solitude.) So this is a 'voyage' made through the night but towards enlightenment and as such a model for Céline of all 'voyages', whose purpose is to teach us dark truths about human behaviour. By the time his mission to Noirceur is complete, Bardamu has travelled a little further into the moral blackness of the night. Hence the name found by Céline for his nocturnal destination: the lily is symbolically the whitest or purest of flowers, but now it has been blackened, its purity is destroyed. This unholy process of denigration lies at the heart of Céline's intentions as a writer: 'One must blacken, and blacken oneself', was his recurrent slogan, as if it were unthinkable for him in his books not to portray the world and its citizens in a far worse light than he knew they deserved.

There is one further question to put about Bardamu's night-ride to Noirceur: why, seen as a 'deliverance', is it 'fictitious' – the French word used is *fictive*? Here I think Céline has brought the idea of fiction in openly, in order to give a deeper, more self-aware sense to Bardamu's comment, by lifting the theme of the voyage on to the plane of the imagination, where it acquires its full resonance and becomes something positive. The 'fictitious' is the agency whereby we are released in imagination from the painful constraints of reality; Bardamu is almost saying, 'My deliverance was through fiction.' But there is a reminder too in his words that such a 'deliverance', being imaginary, can last only for as long as the imagination is working, there can be no final release from reality.

There is a greater literary sophistication than one might have expected in the way in which Céline thus employs the theme of the voyage on a reduced scale, to represent in miniature the larger theme of his novel. The device is one which came to be much used in the hyper-conscious French New Novel of the 1950s and 60s, and is commonly known as the *mise en abyme*, a term taken from blazonry, where it refers to the reproduction, as one element of a coat-of-arms, of the coat-of-arms as a whole. It is exceedingly doubtful that Céline himself knew of the term, even though it had been adopted by his contemporary, André Gide, but it is a striking fact about the *Journey* that such 'voyages within the voyage' as Bardamu's mission to Noirceur are episodes of peculiar intensity (and unreality; this point I will take up again) and peculiarly revealing of what a great deal is contained within the theme of the voyage.

The most compelling example of all such *mises en abyme* is the voyage which Bardamu makes in order to take up his job in west Africa, as a passenger on the good ship *Amiral Bragueton*. This blackly comic episode goes back, interestingly, to the very first piece of prose writing of Céline's to have survived, which is an unfinished story entitled 'Des Vagues', or 'Waves', written on board ship when he was returning to Europe in 1917. 'Des Vagues' is an ill-made but forceful, satirical account of a saloonful of ship's passengers no two of whom are of the same nationality and none of whom shows anything but ill-will towards the others. Faint echoes from it may still be heard in the far more ferocious animosities that mark the voyage of the *Amiral Bragueton*. In this ship's name Céline effects a characteristic conjunction, of the pompous with the bawdy, the second term being framed to mock at the officious dignity invoked by the first. There was, needless to say, no such eponymous mariner as Admiral Bragueton, but a French reader would be quick to see the surname as a derivation from *braguette*, a French word for the 'flies' on a pair of trousers. This burlesque name itself sets the pattern for Bardamu's stormy residence aboard, by promising that as the voyage develops, whatever dignity his fellow-voyagers may originally have possessed will be removed from them – the same promise is endorsed by Bardamu's description of the vessel itself, which is so aged that the owners have removed the plaque recording the date of its construction; it is now kept afloat only by its paintwork. This caustic reduction of something as solid as an ocean-going ship to its skin of paint is all one with Céline's programme for the evacuation of substance from life in order to display its true precariousness.

Bardamu's choice of Africa for the destination of his voyage is presented as a more or less gratuitous one: 'To Africa, said I! The further away it is, the better it'll be!' (P 111 M 104). This is not the brave spontaneity of the adventurer, but the indifference of the desperate escapee. Africa will remove him far enough away from the horrors and perils of war, even if the Africa he promises himself will be, not the 'decorticated' version of it offered by travel agencies but the 'real' continent, 'the one of impenetrable forests, of poisonous exhalations, of unbroken solitude [. . .]' (P 112 M 105) – again, the idea of elsewhere as a place where the voyager can be alone. And like all Célinian voyages, this one proves a further initiation into reality as interpreted by Bardamu. Before the *Amiral Bragueton* even reaches tropical Africa it turns into an extension of this new reality, and gives him a worrying foretaste of the climate and the society into which he is about to be projected. At a given moment, Céline turns up the heat on board, until the temperature is so extreme that a process of liquefaction starts, as the passengers dissolve into sweat but also into an instinctive brutishness, the two kinds of dissolution, physical and moral, being synchronised. The Africa for which Bardamu is heading is simply a macro-climate of Céline's own making, a visionary continent where conditions are such as to bring out the utterly corrupt state of humankind. In the north such a 'reality' may go unseen:

In the cold of Europe, the chaste greyness of the north, you only suspect the cruelty wriggling around inside our brethren, except for the bloodbaths, but their rottenness invades the surface the moment the miserable fever of the Tropics gets into them. That's when they unbutton themselves frantically and the filth takes over and covers us completely. That's biology coming out.   (P 113 M106)

This frantic 'unbuttoning' can be taken literally, bearing in mind the name of the ship on which Bardamu and his 'brethren' are travelling; Céline is nothing if not excremental, in impressing on us his harsh and aggressive 'truths' of biology. The tropical heat is meant for a catalyst, it reveals people as they truly are, putrescent in body and corrupt in soul. In Noirceur-sur-la-Lys, Bardamu reflects that his has been a night of discovery, that all those people he has met with in the course of it have shown him their 'soul'; on the *Amiral Bragueton* it is the same, the sottish passengers congeal into a mass around the ship's bar, and their 'true nature' is set free, 'just like in the war'. The effect of this revelation is to isolate Bardamu, as the solitary individual in possession of the truth about humanity, and his role on board the ship becomes paradigmatic of his role in life generally. His isolation there among so many passengers endows him finally with a moral pre-eminence: as a pariah he can pass judgment on the species.

But there is a price to be paid for such a superiority: Bardamu is not like the other passengers on the ship, and he must suffer for his singularity. He pays the price literally, since he alone has had to buy his own ticket for the voyage; all the others going to West Africa are soldiers, civil servants or teachers whose passage has been paid for by the government. Hence, by a typically perverse reasoning, the hostility he is shown: 'I was the one paying passenger, and the moment that particularity was known, I was found as a result to be singularly shameless, decidedly unbearable' (P 113 M 106). Clearly there is more to 'paying' than we might suppose, if it can have such drastic consequences. But the real 'payment' which Bardamu has made is not his fare to Africa, it is his experience of war, that is, of life, and he is picked upon by the other passengers for the singularity of that harrowing knowledge. At first Bardamu does nothing and says nothing, yet he still enjoys among them 'a disturbing prestige'. Indeed, it is his very privacy which has inflamed the suspicion and resentment of which he fancies he may become the sacrificial victim, until he appeases them by 'disclosing' imaginary sentiments which are the opposite of those he feels.

If the voyage of the *Amiral Bragueton* is in its lurid unreality an episode of true Célinian 'delirium', then the voyage which Bardamu makes on leaving Africa is more delirious still. This time he is literally feverish, and not properly aware of what is happening to him. He travels to New York below decks on a slave-galley named the *Infanta Combitta*, an invention symmetrical with that of the *Amiral Bragueton*, 'infanta' being a Spanish title of rank and the 'bite' so prominent phonetically in 'Combitta' one of many slang words in French for the penis. This second sea-voyage is brief and relatively benign, galley-slave though Bardamu be. Once in America, however, he shows his singularity once more in wanting to jump ship. His fellow rowers see no sense in that:

"He's crazy", they said, "but he's not dangerous." The grub wasn't bad on the *Infanta Combitta*, your mates got flogged a bit, but not overmuch, it was bearable on the whole. Average, as jobs go. And then there was one sublime advantage, you never got fired from the galley and the King had promised them even a sort of small pension for when they were sixty-two. That prospect made them happy, it gave them something to dream about and on Sundays so they could feel free, what's more, they played at voting.   (P 185–6 M 170–1)

The condition of galley-slave is in fact that of the 'average' working man, whose presumed blessings − job security, the promise of a pension, the democratic plaything of the vote − Céline himself found contemptible and insulting to our potential autonomy in life. Bardamu will have no more of a condition which for the born voyager is degrading. The brief episode of the *Infanta Combitta,* casual though it may seem, is one more demonstration that in the *Journey* all such 'voyages' are crucial to the delivery of Céline's most subversive message.

Robinson

Another main focus of unreality in the *Journey* is the forbidding and elusive figure of Robinson, who materialises for the first time during Bardamu's fantastic expedition to Noirceur-sur-la-Lys. Thereafter his reappearances are intermittent though influential, until in the last quarter of the novel he comes to play a leading role in its melodramatic dénouement. Whatever realism Robinson might possess as a character is belied by the arbitrary manner of his repeated introductions into the text, on the battlefield, very briefly in wartime Paris, in the tropical rainforest of Cameroun, and then in Detroit, a jump ahead of Bardamu on each occasion not only physically but also in his cynical understanding of how the world works and how best to exploit it. There is something intentionally devilish in the sinister precedence he is accorded, as if he were the answer to an invocation rather than a contingent human presence. But once Bardamu is back in Paris, that precedence no longer holds; if anything, the positions are now reversed, Robinson becomes a dependent and Bardamu rises to be the dominant figure of the two.

Robinson first introduces himself, in the darkness of the countryside, as Robinson Léon, an inversion (presumably) of surname and given name such as armies insist on. Thereafter, despite their familiarity, he is Robinson for Bardamu far more often than he is Léon. As such he is an anomaly, since Robinson is not a native French name. It is a name well known in France, however, as everywhere in the western world, for that of Defoe's archetypal castaway, and there exists a French verb (reputedly coined by the famously vagrant young poet, Arthur Rimbaud), *robinsonner*, meaning to let the mind wander − or to travel mentally. In a no doubt sardonic reference to which divagations there is in Paris, in the middle of the river Seine, an uninhabited 'island' or glorified sandbank known as the Ile Robinson: suitably, given the location of the Parisian half of *Journey to the End of the Night*, the Ile Robinson is directly facing the suburb of Clichy.

Céline in fact makes of his Robinson a true Parisian, an emanation of the metropolis. He first enters the novel as a disembodied voice sounding in the night, with the cautionary words 'Don't shout so loud!', uttered in 'a very French voice', and is soon reminiscing to Bardamu − incongruously, given their situation − of his life before the war: 'I was even an engraver sort of, but I didn't like that, because of the disagreements, I preferred selling evening papers in a quiet district where I was known, around the Banque de France . . . Place des Victoires if you want to know . . . Rue des Petits-Champs . . . that was my pitch . . .' (P 43 M 44). There is a nostalgia for central Paris in this precise evocation of it, and an assumed complicity between Robinson and Bardamu, as he recalls small, everyday experiences of peacetime in a 'voyage' into the past. Similarly, when Bardamu catches up with him for a third time in the African rainforests, he finds among Robinson's heteroclite stores and possessions two mementoes of Paris, a picture postcard of the Place Clichy, the focal point of the city for Céline in this novel, and a map of the 'North−South' Metro line, which ran from Montmartre to Montparnasse.

The Robinson of the novel might not seem too suitable a

bearer of a name made honourable in literature and resonant in the public imagination by the pluck and enterprise in adversity of the doughty Crusoe. Indeed, he is in one respect the antithesis of Crusoe: where the castaway preserves in alien circumstances the Protestant values traditional to his class, Robinson holds to no values other than those of a fanatical egotism. He too survives in a hostile world, but by the unworthiest of means. There is nothing to be said in his favour, because he seems to have been created by Céline as an ultimate in human turpitude. In the first half of the novel he acts as a tutor to Bardamu in the iniquity of all human dealings. His status, as a strong but occasional force within the story, is signalled at the outset, when we learn that he is not a regular soldier like Bardamu but a 'reservist', the first such that Bardamu has met with. Bardamu, the foolish young man who has once volunteered for the army, has something to learn from a person clearly older and wiser than himself, a former conscript now recalled, not a willing, fulltime soldier. Robinson's voice, which is all there is of him as yet, holds the promise of experience: 'I couldn't see his face, but his voice alone was different from ours, as if sadder, therefore more valid than ours. Because of that, I couldn't help having a bit of confidence in him. That was a little something' (P 41 M 43). It is not often that Bardamu feels confidence in anyone, and that he should feel 'a bit of' it in Robinson – and on the strength of his *voice* – is a portent of the influence over him that this satanic guru will now have.

The immediate example set by Robinson is, in the context of what purports to be the first autumn of the war, monstrous. He speaks up for an elementary kind of pacifism, both cowardly and solipsistic; he is against war for one reason, that he wishes not to be killed but to have as many more years of life as he can. He is on the run, though not through enemy action; his regiment has disintegrated – the process of disintegration is endemic in this novel – after being strafed in error by other French troops. For Céline such an 'error' is a sign not of military incompetence, but of internecine desires in the human race that overstep such facile distinctions as that between friend and foe, or Frenchmen and Germans. The true individual caught up in war, a Robinson or a Bardamu, must be shown as equally at risk from his compatriots as from the official enemy. Robinson's pacifism goes to the extreme of imagining an ideal surrender of his threatened person to the Germans while wearing no clothes at all, so that they would not know from which army he had come, a *reductio ad absurdum* which Bardamu receives as a very practical recommendation. A naked man would no longer be a soldier, not French, nor attributable to any other category of being, he would be neutral, 'like a horse' as Robinson strikingly puts it. (For Céline, animals rank above human beings, morally speaking, as being creatures of rare and beneficent intuitions.)

Robinson's rational cowardice is a model for Bardamu subsequently in the novel, whenever he is under threat, as on board the *Amiral Bragueton*. A grimmer lesson still for him is Robinson's refusal to sympathise with the sufferings of other men – his ability, indeed, to find gratification in such sufferings. Making his escape from the débâcle of his regiment, Robinson has come upon his wounded captain:

He was leant against a tree, the captain, in a right mess! Busy croaking he was . . . He was holding his pants in both hands, spitting . . . He was bleeding from all over rolling his eyes . . . There was no one with him. He'd had it . . . "Mummy! Mummy!" he was whimpering as he croaked and pissing blood too . . . "Stop that!" I said to him. "Mummy! She doesn't give a shit". Just like that, I'll tell you, in passing! . . . Out of the corner of the mouth! . . . He must really have enjoyed that, the bastard! . . . What about that! . . . It's not often you can give the captain a piece of your mind, eh . . .

(P 42 M 44)

Vindictiveness of this order is still shocking for us to imagine, even in a day when our tolerance of such extremities of malevolence has grown far greater, in the doubtful cause of emotional honesty. Robinson's spite is that of the private soldier revelling in the bloody destruction of an officer, it is a gloating recognition that in the ignominious manner of this death the hierarchy of rank and the exploitation of one person by another which goes with it have been violently overturned; the last, ugly laugh is with the no longer subordinate Robinson, who is alive and now, suddenly, because he is no longer submerged in the anonymity of his fellow-soldiers, free. His greatest brutality is the rejoinder inspired in him by the dying officer's instinctive appeal to his mother, the appeal for sympathy. In the bitter world of the *Journey* an appeal of this intensity, made *in extremis*, is worse than wasted, it is sure to be met with outright cruelty, as an emotional imposition to which no other reply is possible. Robinson's cruelty here looks ahead to such rejections as that which Bardamu inflicts on Lola in America, when appealed to for a sympathetic prognosis over her mother's cancer.

Robinson's medium is the night; daylight is alien to him. When he first enters the novel he is indistinguishable from the blackness (of Noirceur), and his preferred job before the war has been selling not morning but evening newspapers. He is met with again in the twilight of the tropical forest, and then in Detroit, where the only work he has been able to find is that of office-cleaner, a member of another nocturnal army, 'a sort of foreign legion of the night'. Back in Paris he is enveloped before very long in the night of blindness, after the failure of his machinations to destroy old Madame Henrouille, and that private darkness is compounded by his consequent insertion into the shared darkness of a crypt, after he has moved to Toulouse with his intended victim, to act as custodian of a collection of mummified corpses. His whole being, his whole history, seem irredeemably dark and negative.

Yet there is more to Robinson than his satanic side; he is a creature of more than the darkness. Reminiscing to Bardamu about his early life, he recalls an episode from thirty years before, when as an eleven-year-old he had been sent out to work as a delivery boy for a luxury shoemaker. While on an errand from the shop he was seduced by a woman customer, an experience from which, by his own account, he has never recovered. At the time he thought his conduct so 'abominable' that he never went back to the shop that employed him. This is a peculiar reaction, even for an eleven-

year-old. The boy Robinson has not sinned, he has been sinned
against. However, any event from his past which leads him into
such wildly uncharacteristic moralising at his own expense as to
describe his actions as 'abominable' is worth our attention. An
element of apparently lasting shame has been added to him,
with his early and untoward initiation into the pleasures of sex.
But it does not seem to have been the sex-act itself which made
him feel shame so much as the memory it left him with of a certain luxurious sensuality, of his having encountered the
pampered body of a woman, and in pampered surroundings.
There is thus an economic aspect to the event: the poor errand-
boy has glimpsed a way of life denied to him by his class. Rather
than an initiation into a world of sexual and monetary
gratification, Robinson's experience has been one of exclusion;
he has been let briefly into the secret of a world that will have no
place for him. And nothing of what he has found in life since
that moment has come up to the expectations then aroused.
Henceforth, reality can never satisfy him. His Fall has been out
of the real and into the imaginary:

Lots of things may have happened subsequently. He had seen con-
tinents, whole wars, but he had never really got over that revelation.
Yet it amused him to go back to it, to tell me about that sort of moment
of youthfulness he had had with the woman customer. "Having your
eyes closed like that, it sets you thinking", he observed. "It goes
past . . . It's like a film-show inside your nut . . ."   (P 326 M 289)

Robinson's blindness, or darkness, is thus in some sense a self-
inflicted one, and far from a negative state. He is speaking here
as a stand-in for the novelist himself; for the one as for the other
the darkness that follows on the closing of the eyes to the reality
around him is richly and satisfyingly peopled. Robinson's own
internal cinema-show may be limited to masturbatory reenact-
ments of a remembered gratification — one which, as he also
recalls, realised for the very first time in his life a pleasure
previously known to him only in imagination — but this one
realisation has been enough to fix in him for life a sense of the
superiority of imagined or remembered pleasures over real
ones. Robinson's bitter pessimism towards the world is that of
a disappointed man, for whom the imagination is both a curse

and a compensation, and the shameful experience to which that pessimism can now be traced back is one, interestingly, that Céline himself may have had, when working as an errand-boy in Paris – certainly it recurs in his second novel, *Death on the Instalment Plan*, and the recurrence shows that, even if such a thing never in fact occurred, the imagination of it was important to Céline.

In the second half of the *Journey* the relationship between Bardamu and Robinson changes. The turning-point comes in Detroit, where Bardamu has expected to find Robinson well established, already master of an environment which he, Bardamu, finds unnerving. Robinson, however, has not mastered it, he is at a loss. His role as precursor is ended. In a rather obscure episode Bardamu attempts to exorcise him from his own life, as a fantasmal influence he can do without. The exorcism takes the form of an outburst of a vicious candour, directed this time at a two-year-old child. Called in to treat this sickly infant, Bardamu is infuriated by its cries and finds himself no longer able to contain all the 'rancour and disgust' he has inside him. He promises his helpless patient a full lifetime of unhappiness to come and brings down on himself the fury of its mother and her parents. He expresses regret for his outburst, and this alone singles the episode out, since Bardamu, like Robinson, does not admit easily to feeling shame. Children, however, are not adults, they call for our kindness. But Bardamu has wanted, by his frankness, to provoke a 'scandal', a 'sort of brutal scene with myself', and in so doing to 'release' himself once and for all from Robinson. What can the logic of this sequence of thoughts be? Only, perhaps, that by doing the most scandalous thing he can think of, something which he feels in *himself* to be scandalous, Bardamu will achieve an absolute of negation, an act both outrageous to others and punitive of himself. Its satisfactory accomplishment would prove that he had no further need of Robinson, his model in these matters.

By the end of the novel Robinson has himself travelled as far as he well can into the night. Having failed a first time to maim or kill Madame Henrouille, he succeeds in the replay, when he pushes her to death down the rickety staircase of their crypt. But it is not in these brazen acts of inhumanity — acts so brazen, they risk nowadays being thought comic — that his eventual importance lies within the scheme of the book. Rather, we need to look at the manner of his own death. After the murder of Madame Henrouille in Toulouse Robinson reappears in Paris, on the run. He is not on the run from the law, however, but from Madelon, the girl who believes that he is willing to marry her. Madelon is the daughter of the woman who sells candles to visitors to the unlit crypt; she is of the family of light, and thus the wrong party for the furiously nocturnal Robinson. ('La Madelon' was the name of a sentimental song which became very popular among French troops in the First World War, so that the Madelon of the novel embodies a memory of the patriotic togetherness of 1914, which is a further disqualification of her as the potential companion of Robinson.)

At the last Robinson stands for an emotional independence which he defends literally to the death. This is a position already crudely stated by him to Bardamu, and stated more crudely still to his prospective bride and her mother in Toulouse, after he has told them that it is his intention, now that his eyes have recovered, to resume his travels. He is enraged by the suggestion that he should first marry and then take Madelon with him:

Hearing that sort of stuff, that upset me. You know me! As if I'd needed a woman to go off to war! Or to come out of it! And in Africa, did I have women? And in America, did I have a woman? . . . All the same hearing them argue like that about it for hours on end, that gave me gut-ache!   (P 453 M 396)

Robinson is, it seems, proud of his celibacy, which is not imitated by Bardamu even if Bardamu, too, is less sexually active than his avowed sensuality would suggest that he ought to be. But even the relation of sex is a dependency. For Robinson marriage is out of the question because it is the exact contrary of travel. The married man will be stuck in one place and will therefore conserve his naive idealism in respect of the human race; whereas the voyager will experience the world fully, will shed his idealism and will comprehend the ubiquity of human malice. Robinson's alarmed reaction to Madelon and her mother in Toulouse leads the way to the dénouement of his story, when he becomes a martyr to his beliefs. His final rejection of Madelon and her love in Paris is, he assures her very scrupulously, not personal but philosophical; he is not refusing her, indeed he thinks rather well of her, he is refusing love as an idea. He has no need of it, it disgusts him. There is a great honesty about Robinson at this moment; he is acting no longer out of cynicism, but on genuine principle. His individualism cannot contemplate the sharing of his life with anyone else.

His punishment, for the honest promulgation of this unfortunate and unsociable principle, is to be murdered, and Robinson's fate manifests Céline's own remarkable need to see the moral outlaw as a figure inviting persecution. The end of Robinson's voyage – it happens in the course of yet one more 'voyage', of a taxi-ride through the suburban streets – foreshadows the end which the novelist later engineered for himself, having invited persecution by the extremism of his attacks before the Second World War on all manner of people, but in particular on the Jews. And after the war, in the full knowledge of what had been done to Europe's Jews in the death-camps, Céline was still able to see himself as a victim of persecution every bit as pitiable as they were. He exulted in the punishment he had called down on himself. And so it is with the enigmatic character of Robinson, who is the sacrifice finally demanded by the community for the injuries that he has done to it.

The voice

The medical thesis which Céline presented in 1924 opens with the words: 'Mirabeau shouted so loud that Versailles took fright', and then breaks into a hectic summary of the French Revolution and the ensuing twenty-five years of conquest and calamity in Europe. All this by way of introducing his hero, the Hungarian doctor, Semmelweis, who was not born until 1818, three years after the fall of Napoleon brought the revolutionary period to a close. Such a preamble might seem out of place, and overblown, but Céline looks on Semmelweis's terrible life-story as all of a piece with the convulsive events of 1789–1815. In peacetime life is as vulnerable as it is in war: this is the lesson of *Journey to the End of the Night*, too. But why start with Mirabeau, a political schemer, at once populist and closet monarchist, who was in fact dead by 1791, long before Europe was turned upside down? Because Mirabeau was an orator, the most famous of his vociferous times, noted for the vehemence and effectiveness of what he said; Céline's brief history lesson in *Semmelweis* would have Europe convulsed seemingly as a consequence of the speechifying of this one thunderous rhetorician.

Céline identifies with Mirabeau, for the good reason that already he could see where his own gifts lay, that it was through the power and carry of his 'voice' that he could hope to influence the world. It suited him to believe that orators such as Mirabeau count among the prime movers of human history. The *Journey* is a novel made in accordance with that belief, it is a 'vocal' novel, a prolonged rhetorical act, delivered in the scandalously distinctive tones of Bardamu. The role of Bardamu's voice is rhetorical in the forensic use of the word. It is an instrument of persuasion, and it is we whom it will try to persuade, into agreeing that his view of the world is the only right one, that this is how reality truly is. He raises his voice towards us, across the space instituted by the printed page, just as Mirabeau once raised his in Paris towards the distant royal palace of Versailles. And Bardamu, like Mirabeau, is looking to have a certain effect, he is looking to make us fearful. The voice for Céline is above all an instrument by whose means to unsettle the mighty, or all those who, like kings and hypothetical readers, exist in a state of unthinking security denied to such troubled souls as himself.

Had he not believed so intensely in the power which the raised human voice may exert on others, Céline would surely have done no writing at all. Write he did, however, plentifully once he had started, and with the utmost care, with a view always to increasing the rhetorical or emotive force of his prose.

He resented anyone who supposed that because what he wrote was so scathing, that it therefore came easily to him; it did not, he wrote and rewrote laboriously, cultivating his written 'voice', 'raising' it in a second sense of that word. But given what he hoped to achieve by its eventual projection, it is not surprising that quite early on in his career, after he had published only two books, the *Journey* and *Death on the Instalment Plan*, he should have abandoned the writing of fiction and taken to publishing long, lyrical and vituperative pamphlets. The urge to persuade others to accede to his own beliefs and anxieties was so unusually strong that the novel seemed the wrong literary genre for him to practice, inviting its readers as it does to interpret whatever messages it carries as at best equivocal dramatisations of the novelist's convictions, never as a forthright statement of them. When roused politically, as he was through the later 1930s, Céline could think only in terms of tracts, of a more obviously direct form of address whereby his opinions would be embodied not in a fictionalised voice such as that of Bardamu, but in a voice identifiable as his own. The *Journey* is in this sense the most conventional of his books; it is the only one in which the narrator takes shape as a presence formally independent of the author.

It is still, though, a thoroughly 'vocal' novel, whose 'spokenness' invests it with great immediacy. Such an immediacy is out of reach for a narrative of the orthodox 'written' kind, which employs a register of language more formal than the one used with such zest and command by Bardamu. The narrative model behind the *Journey* is thus less that of fiction as we are used to it, than that of everyday life, which contains a surprising amount of narration between friends or acquaintances, itself perhaps modelled unconsciously on literary precedent but having also its own, relatively casual but distinctive protocols. Bardamu recounts his story in such a form as to be 'heard' recounting it. He induces us, that is, to attend to him, as if he were present to us. But if he is present to us, the events that he narrates are not, they lie, the earlier of them especially, well in the past, so that the veracity of his narration is undermined by its chronology. This bardic narrator we take to be not altogether reliable, so vividly circumstantial is his recall of his past, but the authority of his voice is thereby increased, since it holds us all the more compellingly for remaking rather than simply recalling the past.

Bardamu's narration emerges explicitly in the novel's opening lines, out of a preceding silence: 'It was like this it began. Me, I'd not uttered. Not a word. It was Arthur Ganate who started me talking. Arthur, a student, a medic him too, a friend. We meet then in the Place Clichy. It was after lunch. He wants to talk to me. I listen' (P 7 M 13). And once so inspired, or ungagged, the hitherto silent Bardamu will not stop talking for some five hundred pages. His implied silence, before his chance meeting in the Place Clichy, we need not take seriously, it is a silence protested and for that reason suspect – Bardamu's rhetorical strategy involves him frequently in playing the reluctant interlocutor, as if having to be forced into speech. But the establishment, here at the start, of camaraderie as the medium in which narration will take place, points to the essential sociability of Céline's way of writing. A 'spoken' novel must be spoken *to* someone, and a novel as resolutely informal as this one must be spoken not to a stranger but to an associate, to someone able to collude in the liberties it will take with the language, someone such as a fellow medical student who will be alert to the specificities of Bardamu's medical experiences. Even the spectacularly morbid themes of the *Journey* demand a similar familiarity or collusion between the interlocutors, because these are not the themes we normally get on to in our conversations with strangers. We, as readers of the novel, are of course strangers to it; we are being *let in* on Bardamu's narration in all its profanity. And the fact that his voice starts to sound in the Place Clichy positions it centrally in terms of the novel's own topography, as a voice of the unregenerate heart of the modern city. It is the voice of an underclass, but also of a civilisation gone cruelly astray.

At the end of the novel, his narration finished, Bardamu withdraws again into silence, in an act of abdication symmetrical with his earlier accession to language: 'The tugboat hooted from a long way off; its summons passed the bridge, one more arch, another; the lock, another bridge, far off, still further . . . It was summoning towards it all the barges on the river, all of them, and the whole town, and the sky and the countryside, and us, it was leading everything away, the Seine too, everything, let's not say any more about it' (P 504–5 M 441). The human voice here gives way to a mechanical one, whose irresistible summons is no doubt towards the ultimate silence of annihilation, that fate which Céline assumes to lie ahead of us all and from the foreknowledge of which we require constant distraction. The river of Paris has become the river of Time, and Time has no very pretty message for us. Like Scheherezade in the *Arabian Nights*, Bardamu's continued existence is ensured only for as long as he can keep talking; his fluent rhetoric is itself condemned eventually to lapse into silence.

Rhetoric plays an ambiguous part in the *Journey*: either it has power over the minds and feelings of those exposed to it, or it has no power, but must yield to the lethal machinations of reality. It is not long before Bardamu, in action at the front line, is reflecting on the sudden fatuity of words when men are being killed all around you: 'I was thinking to myself too (behind a tree) that I'd love to have seen him there, Déroulède, who I'd heard so much about, to explain to me how he'd manage, when he got a bullet right in the bread-basket' (P 12–13 M 17–18). Now Déroulède was another rhetorician, a nationalist tub-thumper who had helped to work up hatred towards the Germans after the traumatic French defeat of 1870. Against the bullets which actually tear and mortify the human body, rhetoric is worse than useless, it is criminal, because it is proffered by those such as Déroulède who, being far behind the lines, are themselves safe from suffering such brutal mortification. The argument hinges, however, on the presumed success of the rhetorician, since if his patriotic words had not been so persuasive he could not be blamed for helping to send young Frenchmen to die pointlessly in battle. Here is the ambiguity which rhetoric has for Céline: it is presumed to work yet also to be horribly inadequate when confronted by the grim facts of life. It is serious enough as a motive force in human affairs, yet not serious in that it is no defence against physical mutilation or death.

Bardamu is thoroughly alive to the effectiveness of words, both for good and for ill. He blames himself, for example, for the murderous dénouement of the story, having precipitated the final argument between Robinson and the affronted Madelon in the taxi:

When all's said and done it was because of me that they talked again and that the argument then instantly resumed, and how. With words we're never sufficiently cagey, they don't seem anything words, don't seem dangerous for sure, puffs of wind rather, little sounds from the mouth, neither hot nor cold, and easily taken back the moment they arrive via the ear, via the enormous limp grey tedium of the brain. We're not cagey of them, words, and trouble comes.

(P 487 M 426)

Was there ever so backhanded a testimony to the effect of words on the course of human life? They work, but how disastrously, when the main effect traceable to Bardamu's own verbal intervention here is the death of a man. But emotive words can, he argues, raise 'tempests', so repeating the exact term used by Céline in *Semmelweis* to describe the historical upheavals that ensued on the oratory of Mirabeau.

Bardamu's reflections here also show where the antidote to rhetoric is to be found, in biology, by reducing language to the physiological processes involved in its utterance and reception. This echoes an earlier passage in the novel, when Bardamu, who feels morally threatened by him, dwells on ways in which to rob the local priest of his dignity and prestige. First he imagines the *abbé* celebrating mass naked, without benefit of vestments and hence of identity (the elemental nakedness aspired to by Robinson when surrendering in wartime), and then, more fundamentally still, he meditates on the degradingly physical aspects of human speech, on the viscous play of the organs in the mouth, or the 'slobbery setting' in which an idealising language is actually produced. This gleeful materialism is more or less acknowledged by Bardamu to be the means of defence against the possibility of enthralment by the rhetoric of the *abbé*, or else of religion itself; so once again, a certain duplicity attaches to the power of words, which is sufficient for an ingeniously vindictive form of defence to have to be mounted against it.

If the realities of biology can thus put paid to the 'voice', that is because the vocal is not natural. The Célinian 'voice' is the creation of art, and often compared by him to the peculiarly emotive art of music. 'My little music' was a favourite description of the prose whose effects he toiled to sharpen, and the power of music as such is made crucially manifest very early on in the *Journey* when Bardamu follows the military band inside the barrack gates, in a moment of naive enthusiasm for which the whole of the rest of his story is his extended punishment. Never again will he be so gullible, thereafter he will recognise rhetoric for what it is. He is no longer so susceptible to it when listening to the mayor of Noirceur-sur-la-Lys, who lectures him on his civic and patriotic duties; he is not susceptible to the enticing picture of the United States painted for him during his convalescence by Lola (it is the memory of her body which subsequently draws him there, not her words); he is not susceptible to the uplifting speeches of the senior doctor at his hospital, whose highest aim is to get his shattered patients fit enough to be returned to the slaughter (this doctor's name, Bestombes, with its graveyard element, undercuts the patriotic encouragement in which he deals). The military band has taught Bardamu all too well: he will beware in future of all rhetoric, whether it is explicitly musical or not, because he knows the dangers it can expose you to.

The parodox, obviously, is that he is himself the most versatile rhetorician of them all. Why should we listen to him, if rhetoric carries a health warning? The answer is that we shouldn't, given the lowering nature of what he has to tell us, but that we cannot help ourselves, such is the artistry with which he has been endowed. The lesson of Bardamu is that it takes a consummate rhetorician to show up other rhetoricians. His is a theoretically self-annulling form of rhetoric,

which ought to neutralise itself by its own success. But only
theoretically self-annulling, for in practice it works. Indeed,
in Bardamu rhetoric is promoted to be a way of living in the
world, of negotiating successfully with a very unfriendly environment. For him to resort to rhetoric is to play the enemy's
game, and in so doing circumvent' their plans for his destruction. This is a lesson taught him in the hospital run by the
dangerously jingoistic Bestombes, whose facility of tongue is
seductive, if not always to the soldiery whose morale it is aimed at restoring, then to the young nurses after whom that
same soldiery lusts. There is another patient in the hospital
who has learnt to play Bestombes's game, Sergeant
Branledore, who ingratiates himself with the establishment,
and in particular the nurses, by opportunistic shouts of the
one word 'Victory!', even though he is utterly cynical as to
the outcome of the war. *Branler* is a French verb meaning
among other things to masturbate while *dore* sounds in-
distinguishably from *d'or*, so the devious sergeant is
presumably meant as a model of how most wisely to react to his
situation of stress – masturbation fantasies are, as we have seen,
an important part of Robinson's strategy for survival and are
clearly likened by Céline to the activity of literary creation.

When he is later imperilled, as an extremely unpopular
passenger on board the *Amiral Bragueton*, Bardamu reveals
his newfound mastery of Branledore's method. His salvation
is ensured through the artful mimicry of the enemy's
language. The cardinal moment of his paranoiac voyage occurs
when he is confronted by a spokesman for the other
passengers, an officer of the colonial army, and challenged to
speak out, 'to enumerate your grievances out loud! . . . To
proclaim what you have been shamefully recounting under
your breath for the past twenty-one days! To tell us in fact
what you are thinking . . .' This is a challenge to which Bardamu
rises nobly:

"Of what abominable slander, gentlemen, have you become the victims?
To go so far as to think that I, in short, your brother should have
persisted in spreading infamous calumnies against gallant officers!
That is too much! It is really too much! And this at the very moment

when these brave fellows, these incomparably brave fellows are ready-
ing themselves, and with courage, to reassume the sacred charge of
our immortal colonial empire!'', I went on. ''When the most
magnificent soldiers of our race have covered themselves in
everlasting glory . . .''   (P 120 M 113)

By means of this obsequious parody, Bardamu's peace is
made and the hostility that had threatened him is neutralised.
But if we enjoy his verbal resourcefulness at this point, and
the abjectness of his capitulation, we should do so guiltily,
because what Bardamu has displayed is also the irresponsibility
of language. His contemptuous effort at mimicry has enabled
him to say things he doesn't mean, to say in this instance
things which are the exact opposite of what we already know
he believes as to the worth of his fellow-passengers. Such an
irresponsibility of voice is pardonable because it is so gross;
had it been subtler, leaving us in doubt as to his true feelings,
it would have seemed more troubling. But the fact is established, that the voice may be used to equivocate when equivocation
is in our interests. I have said that Céline knew something at
least of the teachings of Freud, and among other things the notion that it is good for us to express troubling thoughts that
might otherwise produce unhappiness in us, or harm our rela-
tions with others. There is a parody of the Freudian model of
confession in Bardamu's behaviour on board ship: invited to
bring out into public view the murky thoughts he has been
keeping to himself, he responds by 'expressing' conspicuously
false thoughts the better to save himself. His true confession
he has already made to us. But the false confession has a
therapeutic effect beyond that of merely safeguarding him
bodily, because Bardamu says that as a consequence of this
episode the last remnants of his self-respect have left him and
that he now feels 'infinitely free and light, morally that is'.
This is the release from anxiety which follows from the
realisation that the voice may be freely used, without concern
for truth, in the service of one's own physical security.

The body

Bardamu's vocal flights have as their premise his unholy

pleasure in urging on us the bad news of our mortality. There is much envisaging of death in the *Journey*, and of the biological processes which portend it; his vision is of a reality marked with the sign of its eventual dissolution. It is ironical on Céline's part to bend Bardamu's vital gift for rhetoric in this way to an entirely morbid purpose. The voice that we hear throughout the novel is hugely alive, yet it is intended for our greater discomfort. The 'truths' it passes on to us are those which unsettle Bardamu, the narrator, because they point ahead to the certainty of an everlasting silence: they are the truths of the perishable human body. The voyage to the end of the night carries the voyager from life into non-existence, and that is a calamitous prospect which, this novel insists, we should bear in mind. Only very rarely does Céline seem to be saying that bearing it in mind will make more sympathetic human beings of us; generally, the prospect of non-existence is evoked in order to chasten us without any corresponding wish to reform.

Céline opposes the body not to the mind, but to the 'heart', thus setting up rival scales of values in the novel, the one carnal, the other sentimental. Bardamu the realist stands almost invariably for the carnal values, in the assurance which he has that the other, sentimental kind have betrayed him. The contrast between the two comes sharply out when he first meets Lola, during his convalescence in Paris. Her reasons for coming to France from the United States are presented sardonically: 'She had come to help us save France, she confided to the Manager of the hotel, as far as her feeble strength would allow, but with all her heart!' (P 49 M 50). This fatuous idealism, reported more or less in Lola's own words, is tolerable to Bardamu only because it comes from an athletic American body. His values are other: 'We understood one another right away, but not completely even so, because outbursts of emotion had become thoroughly disagreeable to me. I preferred bodily ones, quite simply. We need to be hugely mistrustful of the heart, I'd been taught that, and how, in the war!' (P 49 M 50).

The heart remains very faintly alive within Bardamu, in the tenderness he shows towards the innocently outgoing age of childhood, or towards animals, or in rare moments of temptation, when he senses he might exchange his hardened self-concern for the warmth of human sympathy. But he has had his one disastrous outburst of emotion, when he was inspired to volunteer for the army. That was a moment of trustingness for which he has been paid out by his terrible exposure to death and the destruction of human bodies in Flanders. It is as a soldier that Bardamu first recognises his singularity in respect of death. Other soldiers appear able to disregard the prospect of their imminent annihilation, whereas he bears it ineradicably in mind. He has no beliefs of any sort with which to hide or lessen its horror, no religion that might let him suppose he has an indestructible soul, no patriotism that might persuade him to die gladly, no cause of any sort to which to make over his individuality. Death, in war as throughout the *Journey*, will mean the irrevocable abolition of his cherished self, which it is Bardamu's fierce wish to defer for as long as possible. Survival in the body is for him the one unarguable good.

Céline takes bloody advantage of the opportunities granted to him by warfare to dramatise the morbidity of his vision. There is nothing either noble or admirable in the individual deaths on which the text elaborates in this early part of the novel; they are the brutal termination of a life, and the messier that termination is the more keenly Bardamu's point is made, that we are as human beings nothing but our bodies. The integrity of his own body becomes his one imperative on the battlefield and the rationale for his cowardice. He cannot tolerate the idea that it might be violated. Subsequently, Bardamu tells Lola that he will refuse cremation when he dies, because he would rather be a skeleton than a pile of ash, skeletons still bearing some resemblance to a living body and being somehow more propitious as a starting-point were there a question of resurrection. This is not meant facetiously by Céline; there is something profound at stake for him here. The skeleton has one redemptive asset, it is hard, and it has form, it is much less subject than the flesh that once covered it to the process of corruption. To that extent it is a mortuary emblem reassuring rather than frightening.

To preserve a human form in death, however tenuously, is to remain a little longer on the side of the living. The 500-year-old bodies on display to tourists in the crypt in Toulouse have for Bardamu when he sees them a curious, intermediate status, 'Neither quite skin or bone, or clothed . . . A bit of all that together merely . . .' (P 387 M 340). They are not yet quite dust and 'asked for nothing better than to enter into Eternity'. But that final step out of existence is not possible for as long as they keep the semblance of a living body. Meanwhile, they can fulfil their ancient role of reminding the living of the inanimate state to which their own bodies must inescapably come. Immediately before going down into the crypt Bardamu has been wrestling amorously with Madelon, winding himself around her body 'Like a true maggot of love' – in a scene out of some hortatory medieval fresco, with its juxtaposition of lust and mortality. And the maggot (*asticot*) for Céline is the creature that connects the two, the *Journey* containing any number of references to these busy and repulsive agents of our posthumous erosion, which may, as with 'the maggot of love', be invoked in the midst of life as distasteful heralds of finality.

The novel is marked regularly by incidents in which the healthy and reassuring firmness of the human body is lost, to be replaced by bodies tending to a state of shapelessness or liquefaction. I have quoted already the effects of the tropical heat on the passengers of the *Amiral Bragueton*, who in their newly and obsessively liquid environment 'moved limply between the decks, like squid at the bottom of a bathtub of unsavoury water' – Céline having picked on the squid as the most unpleasantly amorphous of submarine presences. But it is in wartime that Bardamu is faced with the most gruesome evidence of how the normally solid human body may be made to show what it is made of, and so lose its consistency. Within a few pages of the start of the novel he witnesses the bloody disintegration of two men:

The two of them were embracing for the minute and for always, but the cavalryman no longer had his head, nothing but an opening above the neck, with blood gurgling and bubbling inside like jam in a saucepan. The colonel had his belly opened, and was pulling a vile face about it [. . .] All this meat was bleeding tremendously together.   (P 17 M 22)

In this grotesque 'embrace' of two bodies there is a premonition of the erotic episode of Bardamu and Madelon in Toulouse − in this instance the bodies are those of an officer and of a private soldier, so that their new configuration in death abolishes the hierarchy to which they had belonged in life, again as in some medieval invocation of the Great Leveller.

The typical callousness of Bardamu's description here is meant to jolt us into the realisation that we are all of us simply meat. The officer commanding in the sector where Bardamu is serving is General des Entrayes, a name that to a French ear has the sound of *entrailles*, meaning 'intestines' but also, less concretely, 'bowels', as a seat of strong emotion interchangeable with the 'heart' (cf. English 'bowels of compassion'). In the colonel's fatal stomach wound we get a literal spilling of the *entrailles*, but also the death of compassion in Bardamu, who in future will take refuge from strong feeling in the very cruelty of his description of the event. If men are just 'meat', he need not feel for them. The deaths of the colonel and the cavalryman lead on, two pages later, to one of Céline's most hauntingly visceral descriptions, of a field behind the front line in which army butchers are dismembering the regimental meat supply. The sight of so many dripping innards and puddles of blood is too much for Bardamu, he passes out and has to be carried off on a stretcher. (An 'exemplary nausea' the French critic Jean-Paul Richard calls this, in a brilliantly revealing essay on the *Journey*, which draws attention to its consistent imagery of deliquescence.) It is a heavy irony, of course, that Bardamu, unmoved as he has been by the blowing to bits beside him of two fellow human beings, should be caused to faint by what is nothing other than the humdrum mode of butchery followed daily in any city abattoir. This army abattoir, however, is incongruous, it is in the open air and Bardamu's description of it is all the more striking for the fact that the entrails and the blood are soaking into the grass of the field, like so many carnal pollutants. This is Céline bringing into the open a practice which normally takes place sufficiently in secret for us to ignore its existence. The alfresco abattoir repeats the theme of the desecration of once shapely flesh, as well as helping to reveal the awful biological truth of things, that animal feeds on animal.

Bardamu is unique and isolated as a soldier for being in possession of this truth. He possesses it because he has imagination; a faculty denied to those around him. His colonel had no imagination and that is why he died; had he had some, he would not have remained where he was and been hit by a German shell. Those with imagination, that is, *move*, they are the voyagers. But if the imagination is a saving faculty, a means of mental escape, when we must otherwise capitulate to the terrors of reality, it is also the faculty by which we recognise those terrors to *be* terrors. Without imagination they are nothing. This is especially true of the worst fact of all, of the omnipresence of death. Bardamu's reflections on this, amidst the carnage of war, are brief but definitive: 'When you've no imagination, dying's nothing really, when you do have some, dying's too much. That's my opinion. I'd never understood so many things all at once' (P 19 M 23). The imagination of death is the persistent theme of *Journey to the End of the Night*. As a survivor of war, Bardamu must endure what he calls 'a sort of deferred death agony, lucid, in good health, in which it's impossible to understand anything other than absolute truths . . .' (P 52 M 53). Such is the expression of his anguished carnality, but anguished it is, because there is unhappiness in Bardamu, the heart still makes demands on this resolute materialist (the heart and its demands is the last of my six themes here).

In his life of Semmelweis, Céline quotes his hero (whether accurately or not hardly matters) to the effect that destiny had chosen him to be the 'missionary of the truth over the measures that need to be taken to avoid and to combat puerperal fever'. That truth was a materialist one: puerperal fever occurred because of faulty hygiene and not, as

Semmelweis's adversaries argued, from psychological causes. Medical students went straight from the dissection of dead bodies to the examination of women in labour, so infecting them and demonstrating as it were the contagion of death. In the *Journey* it is the same. Bardamu is the medical student who passes from the dissecting room, or abattoir of war, to the labour wards of Paris. Once he is in practice as a doctor, obstetrics looms large in what is asked of him, and the obstetrics of miscarriage, not of successful birth. In these medical episodes he displays the same brutal acquiescence in the afflictions of the human body as he had done in wartime. One patient, an unmarried mother, has just had her third backstreet abortion and is found bleeding, possibly to death, in her bedroom, because her mother is too ashamed to let her be moved to the hospital; Bardamu comes and passively looks on, comparing the girl's haemorrhaging uterus to the severed neck of the colonel in Flanders (a textual slip: it is the cavalryman whose head is blown off). In a second case not many pages later another woman is miscarrying, and bleeding every bit as freely as the first. In either instance, it is the escape of blood, or of bodily fluids, which dominates the description and which Bardamu does nothing at all to try and stem. He accepts tacitly that this is how it must be, that human substance must dissolve unstoppably.

There is a point in the *Journey* where Céline comes oddly close to dramatising this as his *own* obsession. Baryton, the asylum-keeper, has been asked to care for one patient who is a writer and whose mind has been 'wandering', which is what minds are best off doing according to the writer Céline. This particular writer's mania takes the form of going around shouting the words 'They're liquidating! They're liquidating! [*on liquide!*]' His family believe that these mysterious cries are a further proof of his literary genius, but the materialist Baryton knows better, that the writer has trouble passing water because of a blockage in his bladder. This is the truth of his patient's state, but the family will not accept it; Baryton must yield, since business comes before truth, but then families for Céline are a source of nothing but falsehood, and above all of such falsehoods as this, which shift the locus of disease from the body into the mind and so shield us from the recognition of our bodily fragility. Céline's concern with liquefaction is here shown to be, not a pathological fantasy but a rational acknowledgement of the material facts of our existence.

To think about the body is thus to think about death, the conclusion to which all thought leads, according to Bardamu; hence his cheerless verdict, reached in a hotel room in New York: 'The truth of this world is death'; words repeated, all but verbatim, from Céline's then unpublished play, *L'Eglise*. Whatever denies or conceals this truth is inevitably a falsehood. But if life is inescapably a 'deferred death-agony', it might seem sensible for someone so lucid in this knowledge as Bardamu to anticipate nature and kill himself. Surprisingly, the question of suicide is scarcely raised in the *Journey*. It is invoked by Bardamu, only to be pushed perfunctorily aside, on this same occasion, in New York, when he admits, 'I've never been able to kill myself.' After which he leaves his hotel room and goes down into the street, 'that little suicide' (P 200 M 183). In what sense a descent into the streets can be a suicide in miniature is unclear; unless he means that in the anonymity and hostility of the populous city selfhood is lost, that only in the fullness of a solitary self-possession can we be properly alive. But Bardamu remains characteristically passive in awaiting rather than precipitating the conclusion of his own life.

Nor are other material objects allowed to be exempted from this downward, entropic course. Another of Bardamu's hopeless cases in Clichy is that of the husband Henrouille, a paragon of petty bourgeois economics who has been saving up for fifty years in order to buy a house. We do not expect Céline to show sympathy for a man so fixated on fixation. In attendance at Henrouille's death-bed, Bardamu is first of all struck by the way in which objects in the bedroom, familar to him from his earlier visits there when treating the injured Robinson, have changed over time:

Things, they're different when you come upon them again, it's as if they had a greater strength to enter more sadly into us, still more deeply, more gently than in the past, to melt [*fondre*] into the sort of death that's slowly forming in us, day by day, indolently, and that we train ourselves every day to defend ourselves against a bit less than the day before.   (P 373 M 328)

This lyrical process of melting, or of fusion — the verb *fondre* recurs many times in the *Journey*, in a great variety of contexts — whereby the material adjuncts of our lives are absorbed into our bodies and so share in its fate, is a remarkable extension of the dissolution of matter, remarkable if also unpersuasive, when most of us would part company on this with Céline and see things in their stubborn hardness and externality as lastingly resistant to any such 'melting'. But Bardamu's reflections are the prelude to his long and predictably cruel description of Henrouille's death:

I listened to his heart beating, a matter of doing something appropriate, the few gestures expected of you. It was running behind his ribs, you might have said, his heart, shut in, running after life, in jerks, but jump though it might, it wouldn't catch life up. It was done for. With all that stumbling, it was soon going to start putrefying [*il chuterait dans la pourriture*], his heart, all juicy, in red and foaming like an old squashed pomegranate.   (P 374 M 329)

The ultimate destiny of the body could not be more barbarically pictured. The posthumous imagination of 'dust to dust', or of 'ashes to ashes', we are accustomed to, but that is too dry, too wholesome a prospect to appeal to Céline; he must have a moist putrescence — the noun *pourriture* is another of the novel's key-words — and imagine it at work on the most eagerly idealised of our body's organs, the heart. But the very luxuriance of Bardamu's materialism in such passages as this is a clue that there remain within him sentiments of another, positive and compassionate sort which he is fighting to exclude. And with those sentiments there goes an altogether contrary, positive view of the human body, as a source of sexual and aesthetic pleasure. Through the body Bardamu is able, too, to have an experience of community.

Imagination

Were Céline concerned in the *Journey* exclusively with the

propagation of a funereal philosophy, then this could not be the incomparably lively book that it is. The energy, humour and verbal accomplishment of the writing are at odds with the morbidity of its themes. One can hang moreover on the voice of the often monstrous Bardamu without finding him morally repellent, for his callousness is so extreme as to set him outside the sphere of serious ethical discussion; it is more likely to amuse by its insolence than to appal by its inhumanity. He is in revolt against the accepted pieties of his society but he has nothing with which to replace them, and the great theme of death is itself introduced dialectically, as a solitary and anxious man's response to the insouciant lives which he observes being lived around him. Like any such prophet of doom, Bardamu depends for his livelihood on the perceived superficiality and myopia of everyone but himself. In this sense other people keep him going, by constantly feeding his misanthropy. Bardamu is not observing other people, however, he is imagining them; he is not a realist but a visionary, and the imagination therefore is for him a vital and sustaining force. As a character he is proof that the seemingly sterile obsession with death can be a most creative thing: an inspiration.

Bardamu's splendidly vigorous and imaginative narration is thus on the side of life, and in profound contradiction of the 'truth' which it wishes us to share in; it proves that death is not all, since there is one force at least in the world which works against death. And the text itself is there in the end to manifest the victory of the countervailing force, standing finally as a magnificent rebuff to the silence which is the medium of death. Bardamu knows from the start that as a narrator he is engaged on a duplicitous task. In L'Eglise he had first delivered his aphorism about death being the truth of life in a particular context: he is asking himself whether he should tell a woman in New York that her doctor husband has died in Africa. He is the bearer of an unwelcome truth; but need he pass it on? Very elliptically, he envisages the alternatives: 'The truth in this world, y'know is death. Life's an intoxication, a lie. It's ticklish and quite indispensable. Dying's like breathing. Suppose I told her nothing?' Again, in the *Journey*, when Bardamu repeats his aphorism, the alternative of mendacity is immediately raised: 'The truth of this world is death. We must choose, to die or to tell lies. I've never been able to kill myself' (P 200 M 183). The logic of this appears to be: death is the truth of life, being its natural termination, but the notion of 'truth' brings language, or the 'voice', into the picture, because truths are forms of words, and words can as easily be false as truthful. The possibility exists for Bardamu in *L'Eglise* to spare the doctor's widow his bad news, which he is tempted to do because she is a woman of obvious and for him seductive vitality. For the more mature Bardamu of the *Journey* such a possibility would be a sign of weakness; his logic is different: the alternative facing any human being, in the dismal conditions of life on earth, is to die or to tell lies, and since he has not been able to kill himself he has chosen to lie.

Since Bardamu is before all else the appointed revealer of the 'truth', something seems to have gone askew with this syllogism. But all that has gone askew is that he has defined his role in the Célinian scheme without going on to show what is truly distinctive about it. To die or to tell lies are not genuine or equal alternatives, when to die is to pass beyond language altogether. Only by remaining alive is it possible to establish the truth of death, by associating oneself with the chorus of the untruthful. Bardamu will be the odd voice out in that chorus, an interloper who will appropriate its devices for the communication to the world of his own dire conclusions.

This singularity cannot be carried too far, however; Bardamu is too ambiguous a figure to be fully accommodated within such a dichotomy. He is an artist as well as a soothsayer, and he knows it. He even knows what we know, as readers of the *Journey*, that soothsaying may itself contribute to making life more bearable and so collude with the practices of mendacity with which it appears to be in conflict. Bardamu's ambiguity of role becomes inevitable once he admits that he, uniquely, has the faculty of imagination, and thus the living power of transforming by a false representation of it the reality which he finds around him. The imagination which in war has made the idea of his death intolerable to him is a truly positive force, it produces *movement* in the mind and to move, as we know from the fate of the unimaginative colonel, is, if not finally to escape, then at least to defer one's prospective annihilation.

It is remarkable now to think that Céline's means and intentions as a writer should once have been mistaken for those of a realist, when there is such conspicuous evidence from within the text of this, his first published book, to the contrary, that he had quite other intentions. Bardamu is a character designed to press mendacity into the service of the truth, or to apply imagination to brute life so as to procure a provisional relief from its terrors. He rejects the major illusion of realism, which is that any one perspective on the world may stand for all perspectives, since what is 'out there' is the same for everyone. Bardamu's perspective on things is unashamedly his own, and its very vigour is evidence that, unlike the perspective of realism, it is not going to be dictated to by what it sees. What counts is his *idea* of the world, whose importance for him only increases with the knowledge that ideas of the world cannot change the world, because reality is impervious to them.

'Life's an intoxication': the sense Céline is giving to these enigmatic words starts to grow clear. Without some mitigation of its 'truth', such as alcohol may supply, life is not to be borne – not for nothing does the prototype Bardamu of *L'Eglise* run his medical practice from the local bar. But the later Bardamu, like Céline himself, is no friend of genuine intoxication, seeing alcoholism as an avoidable scourge of the urban working-class. Less physically ruinous ways need to be found of reconciling human consciousness with the human condition. And this is where the imagination enters, with its formidable powers of distraction from reality. The imagination can lead us into a state of blessed 'delirium' (Céline's own favourite term for it). This 'delirium' is a willed, self-conscious condition which the writer can achieve in his concentration on his art and can induce in his readers if his art succeeds. In that sense, it is a communal state, in which minds can be brought to meet. Céline has a second favourite term for it, more literary this time, and less pejorative − delirium is not a state of mind we should want to be in: of *féerie*, or 'enchant-ment'. His *féerie* is not some mawkish elfin kingdom, but an explicitly fantastic yet consoling vision, coloured − as in the title he used for one of his postwar books, *Féerie pour une autre fois* − by nostalgia for an age that has passed.

There are scenes of *féerie* in the *Journey*, introduced so stealthily that they may easily go unrecognised, or be mistaken for realism. Consider the description which Bardamu gives of the town of Noirceur-sur-la-Lys, once he comes close to it after his solitary ride through the night:

It must have been around two hours after midnight, hardly more, when I reached the crest of a small hill, at a walk. From there I suddenly saw down below rows and more rows of lighted gas-lamps and then, in the foreground, a railway station all lit up with its carriages, its buf-fet, but no sound coming up from it though . . . Not a thing. Streets, avenues, lamp standards, and still more parallel lines of lights, whole districts, and then the rest round about, nothing but blackness, the void, avid around the town, which was all stretched out, on display in front of me, the town, as if it had been lost, all illuminated and spilt out right in the middle of the night. I got off and sat on a small hump to gaze at it for a long moment.(P 40 M 42)

This is not a plausible description of a small town in the battle-zone. The place is too formal, too lit up, too empty, too silent, too unmarked by warfare. Noirceur is very clearly a vision and its effect on Bardamu is to make him sit to observe it, to place him in the sedentary role of the artist. What he sees, looking down on it from his raised viewpoint, is like the archetype of a town, a dream-place, hospitable for the brightness of its illumination and for the invitation to the voyage represented by its railway-station, yet also sinister for being without movement or inhabitants. It is as if Noirceur 'had been lost', says Bardamu. He has been sent officially to find out whether the place has fallen to the Germans, but that surely is not how we should read 'lost' here; rather, it has been lost to a more serious enemy; Time. Life has withdrawn from a setting expressly designed for it and yet the town is not in darkness, quite the reverse, it is a meticulously lit apparation that contradicts the darkness, the 'void' all around it; it is a stage-set, only without actors and with an audience of one. The ambiguousness of Noirceur by night is that of art itself for Céline, or of the imagination, which can likewise light up the darkness in which we must travel but can contain nothing more than the immaterial semblances of real bodily life. The vision of Noirceur may be likened to other scenes in the *Journey*, such as the conflagration in the rain-forest when Bardamu sets fire to the hut he has inherited there from Robinson. This spectacle at once recalls to him a great fire he was taken to see as a small boy in Paris by his uncle Charles − 'the one who was such a good singer of ballads'; this brief commendation surely puts Uncle Charles on the side of art, and of 'romance' − in the year 'before the Great Exhibition', i.e. 1899. That event, I have said, was for Céline a watershed, the end of an imaginary golden age, and there can be no question but that Bardamu is a visionary who looks always behind him when he allows his imagination to travel, towards an age that is uniquely satisfying because it no longer exists.

Many times in his life, talking about his work, Céline said that he dealt there in 'phantoms'. In so saying he was being scrupulous about the nature of his art rather than dismissive of its seriousness; literature can only ever deal in phantoms. But phantoms come to us from the past, they are reminders of what has been, or more particularly of *those who* have been. The *Journey* has in it only one explicit 'vision', which occurs when Bardamu is up one night on the hill of the Sacré Cœur in Montmartre, mixing with the urban crowds in search of 'gaiety'. His girl-friend of the day is with him, and she is drunk, like so many of those around them. Bardamu himself is not drunk, he never is, or not on alcohol, for he has no need of drink in order to accede to the 'intoxication' of life. He can readily enough get high on imagination. Here, on the heights of Montmartre, close by the cemetery of Saint-Pierre, he has a vision of aerial squadrons of the local dead, winging their way northwards and constituting finally an 'abominable débâcle' as they are joined by all the dead from other centuries. They make a weird counterpoint to the more ordinary festivities of Montmartre, but this is Bardamu's preferred form of festivity. It ends facetiously, somewhere over England, where the dead are harder to see because of Albion's everlasting fogs. The vision, needless to say, is private, available to Bardamu alone, for he has the knack of being able thus to summon up the normally invisible dead: they can only be seen, he declares, 'from inside and with the eyes nearly closed'. By this one small phrase Céline as it were naturalises Bardamu's 'vision', rather than allowing it to evolve seamlessly from the more or less objective description of Montmartre. What is deceptive about such explicitness is that it marks this one hallucinatory episode off from the rest of the novel, as if fiction were not by its very nature hallucinatory in the sense of being an inward experience continuous with Bardamu's vision of the dead. On this occasion the visionary has to half-close his eyes in order to shield them from the over-bright lights of the streets, which is to exchange a public means of illumination common to all for a private one, peculiar to himself. The mental lighting, as with the vision of Noirceur-sur-la-Lys, has to be adjusted, turned down or turned up, but in some way privatised.

At other moments Céline links this switching of the mind from a perception of the real to the imagination of the unreal with the beneficent role in twentieth-century life of the cinema. Like alcohol, or writing, films can take our minds off things. For Céline they are a branch of medicine, of that metaphorical kind which actually works, unlike the medicine practised by physicians. Parapine, the research scientist who; when Bardamu first meets him, is uselessly growing microbes at the Institut Bioduret, reappears in the novel as an assistant at Baryton's asylum (his name is one more evidence of Céline's bawdiness, *pine* being a French slang term for penis; intriguingly, when penicillin was first used in France it was jocularly know as *pine à Céline*, though whether this was meant as a salute to the writer I have not been able to find out). There his principal job is taking disturbed patients to the cinema, as a part of their tranquillizing regime. But he has a second string to his therapeutic bow:

In this House, Parapine was in charge not only of the lunatics' trips to the cinema, but on top of that he looked after the sparks. At fixed times, twice a week, he set off veritable magnetic storms above the heads of the melancholics who had been assembled for the purpose in a tightly sealed, pitch black room. Mental sport in fact and the realisation of a bright idea of his employer's, Doctor Baryton.   (P 415 M 362)

These two eccentric therapies are not simply satire, or meant to make of Baryton that stock figure of fun, an alienist who is himself not quite right in the head. There is a serious side to them. Céline believed genuinely in the power for mental good of the cinema, and Parapine's spark-shows are only a slightly more fanciful version of modern ECT. 'Mental sport' is what we all of us require, or those of us who feel acutely 'alienated' from reality, and it is what Bardamu himself as a narrator is providing, a *féerie* that will help us to endure our lot. Baryton the mind-doctor is, I have earlier suggested, a very Bardamu-like figure, an accomplished and impassioned talker, and on themes dear to Céline's heart: on the destructive twentieth-century mania for progress and on the tyranny of families. But for all his oratory, he cannot, according to Bardamu, 'sublimate' his anxieties, hence his need to make his escape from them by abandoning his asylum. (Before he goes, he takes English lessons from Bardamu, implying that not until he has been thus further initiated into the command of language is he fit to become a Célinian voyager). Bardamu's role has been to attend on, and in great measure to assist, Baryton's increasing abstraction from the world around him, and when his employer at last cracks up, he comments: 'He was no sort of musician, Baryton, so he had to overturn everything like a bear, to be done with it' (P 427 M 373). Musical by name but not sufficiently musical by nature: had Baryton been more of a musician he would presumably have adapted himself better to his circumstances, 'music' being that hard-earned fluency of language through which Bardamu has saved himself.

Baryton might also have done well to go to the cinema with his patients, or with Bardamu, who has had much benefit from it. Solitary and disorientated in New York, he is temporarily restored by the movies, and able to endure a few days more adrift in a hostile city. The satisfactions he gets from the cinema are primarily erotic: in this instance he is offered 'A blonde who had unforgettable tits and nape to her neck . . .', while later, in Paris, after he has given up his medical practice and is loose in the city, in search of work and of human company, it is in the Tarapout that he finds it, a cinema which employs a troupe of English dancers. Here Bardamu is laughably employed playing the role of a 'pasha', but for all his casual lasciviousness, he is less a consumer of sex than an imaginer of it; the forms of his sexual gratification are in keeping with his status as visionary. In Detroit, in the brothel where his girl works and where there is much trade on a Saturday evening when the healthy young baseball players come in search of pleasure, Bardamu finds his pleasure differently: he sits there writing. He has found how much satisfaction is to be got not from doing but from imagining that you are doing; he is Robinson, recalling the episode of his sexual initiation as a young boy: 'It's like a film-show inside your nut . . .'

Sympathy

Imagination is the faculty by which Bardamu is first separated from the life around him and then reunited with it, even if in his eventual representation of it that life has been harshly denatured, to accord with the 'lucidity' of his independent vision. For no matter to what end it is used, the imagination restores a certain community with the species, and the blackly imaginative Bardamu is not the altogether pitiless student of humankind which it often seems he would like to be. He hates, he mocks, he condemns, yet sympathy is not dead in him. He feels it for the poor, among whom he numbers himself: for the ample class of the *miteux*, who have no money and no *amour-propre*. This, however, is an abstract sympathy; the poor people whom Bardamu actually meets are not spared his misanthropic gaze. He is on their side only because, being in want, they are experiencing the true precariousness of life. If Bardamu is against money, it is for the doubtful — and quite apolitical — reason that money is a distraction, since those who have it are blind to the insecurities of the human condition. The opposition between moneyed and unmoneyed in the *Journey* is also one between remembering and forgetting: the poor cannot but remember how things are in the world; they do not have the resources to forget, and since Bardamu's own rhetoric is aimed at bringing about such remembrance, he will use poverty for his own philosophical purposes.

But there is another, less abstract sympathy alive in Bardamu: for an honest sensuality. This is embodied in women, in a number of young women, but also, more curiously, in two older ones: in Mme Hérote, the profiteering shopkeeper who has taken advantage of the war to turn her Paris lingerie business into a brothel and who Bardamu approves of for her earthiness, her 'rough, stupid and precise appetites'; and in old mother Henrouille, whom he sympathises with for being a furious egotist, as lucid as himself in reviling the falseness of society and so fluently spiteful in her old age that she revels in showing tourists her collection of corpses. Mainly though, it is young women that Bardamu admires, for the exemplary sensuality of their bodies. Lola, Musyne, the teenage Miss Mischief, Molly, the troupe of English dancers at the Tarapout cinema, Tania, Sophie, these are exceptional figures physically speaking in a book so given otherwise to the depiction of failed or failing bodies, and so marked by the obsession of its author with all forms of deliquescence. They have bodies desirable for their firmness and their athleticism, which are sure, tangible values for Bardamu. These are, quite simply, imaginary bodies, and it is against their ideal carnality that we should measure the degeneration of the novel's many other bodies. They have the power to *move* Bardamu, to set his mind free, which is why he is able more than once to liken them to ships. The last body of the series, that of Sophie, so named presumably to make her recognisable as a bearer of wisdom, is the most lyrically idealised of them all in the grace and suppleness of its movements: she is just the image Bardamu, the mental voyager, needs, 'A three-master of tender joy, en route for the Infinite' (P 472 M 414).

Bardamu commends the sexual relation because he has nothing to fear from it, it commits him only briefly and superficially to another human being, and asks nothing of him emotionally. It is thus not in contradiction to the extreme mistrust which he repeatedly endorses as the safest attitude for us to have towards our own kind if we want to survive in the world. The fear of others is in fact Bardamu's inspiration, fear not just as a feeling but as a motive force. In wartime fear makes him into a practising coward; his distinctiveness as a soldier lies not in his feeling afraid but first, in his being as afraid of his own side as of the enemy, and secondly, in exhibiting and acting on his fear rather than concealing it. His fear is creative, for out of it there comes fiction.

This derivation can be traced textually, in an episode of Bardamu's convalescence when, with Lola, he visits the Bois de Boulogne and the racecourse at Longchamp, where he pretends to recall the picturesque scene there on race days, even though he has never in truth been to the races. Here invention, nostalgia and the seduction of his listener are closely mixed. From Longchamp the two of them go to the park of Saint-Cloud, where a fairground from before the war is still in place, but closed for the duration and deserted. Its first effect, like that of Noirceur by night, is hallucinatory, as well as nostalgic: the fairground is another empty stage-set. Action then follows. Amongst the stalls is a shooting gallery, the Stand des Nations, with some odd painted targets for marksmen to aim at: a wedding party, a town-hall with tricolour flying, a regiment of soldiers on the march. These are the targets, or rather values − the family, patriotism, the military − peculiarly hateful to Bardamu, for whom the sight of this abandoned sideshow is highly emotive. He suddenly imagines he is himself a target, to be shot at once again here just as he had been in the front-line: 'I felt very strange. It's even from that moment on, I believe, that my head became so difficult to keep quiet with its ideas inside' (P 59 M 59). This first, catalytic moment of 'delirium' is followed by an outburst in a crowded restaurant, where he shouts out that he is being shot at and urges everyone to take cover. He is

removed in handcuffs by the gendarmerie. The diagnosis of
the authorities is that Bardamu is 'in fever', that he has been
driven mad by fear, but what we, as readers of the novel,
might say is that he has been turned by fear into a 'visionary',
a man who 'sees Things', unable thereafter to keep the tur-
bulent ideas inside his head to himself. He publishes them to
a crowded room and, be it noted, the forces of order at once
descend on him, because Céline needs to believe that Bardamu's
offensive 'publication', like his own, is punishable.

Nor is this the only time that Bardamu is inspired by fear-
fulness. The final showdown with his hostile fellow-
passengers on board the *Amiral Bragueton*, 'those fantastic
passengers' as he revealingly calls them (I would be tempted
to translate it as 'fantasmal passengers'), opens with one of
the novel's many truculent maxims: 'We're never sufficiently
afraid.' There follows the account of Bardamu's humiliation,
and the loss of his last shreds of self-respect in the fluent
deference with which he capitulates to his enemies. But under
this duress he has again become wonderfully free of tongue,
and far from killing off his *amour-propre*, his parody of self-
abasement in fact bolsters it, by showing what a master he is
of a saving rhetoric. His triumphant surrender is his revenge
for what he has been made to suffer. Bardamu thus needs his
fear, it is what creates him as a 'voice'. Even as a doctor he
needs it, because the practice of medicine too in the *Journey*
rests on a dialectic between fear and revenge. In conversation
with Bardamu in Paris, Robinson says, out of character one
might at first think, that what he would like to have been in
life was a male nurse. But he has a starkly Robinsonian
reason for such an ambition:

Because when men are healthy, y'see, they scare you, that's for
sure . . . Especially since the war . . . I know what's in their
minds . . . They don't always realise it themselves . . . But I know
what's in their minds . . . When they're upright, they're thinking of
killing you . . . Whereas when they're sick, they're less frightening,
that's for sure . . . You can expect anything, I tell you, when they're
upright.   (P 306 M 273)

The doctor, therefore, or the nurse, is in a position of safety *vis-à-vis* humanity, on which he attends at those times when its destructive powers are muted. Better to deal with people only when they are lying down. The extraordinary logic of this is that medicine emerges as the most comfortable vocation for those, like Bardamu, of a fearful disposition, who in their attendance on the sick have the pleasure of triumphing over human beings who in all other circumstances would fill them with mistrust. Indeed, the anxious doctor's revenge is complete: not only are his formerly fearsome patients now innocuous, they themselves are in fear, of pain and of death. This reversal is the very 'gimmick' Bardamu has been looking for in the days before qualifying as a doctor, when experiencing such rejections as that by Lola in New York:

"Buck up, Ferdinand," I repeated to myself, to keep myself going, "if you're kicked out all the time, you'll surely hit on it in the end, the gimmick that scares them all so, all those bastards however many of them there are and which has to be at the end of the night. That's why they don't go to the end of the night!"   (P 220 M 200)

In this ignoble way, the doctor gets his own back, by reducing others to his own state of vital insecurity through his potent reminders to them of their mortality.

But there is more to Bardamu than this ugly *Schadenfreude*. We can assume that here particularly, in the practice of medicine, the great 'blackener' has something honourable to hide. Indeed, his turpitude would make no sense did it not contradict the standard view of medicine as a generous vocation, as practised by those who feel an urge to relieve the afflictions of the body. Egotism as seemingly invulnerable as Bardamu's is doubly suspect when it is exercised in places where we would expect to meet its opposite, an active sympathy. His despicable behaviour in wartime is itself egregious because it conflicts with obvious ideals of comradeship and readiness for self-sacrifice. War by its nature is a potential theatre of altruism, but in the *Journey* altruism is made ridiculous when it features in the jingoistic preachings of doctor Bestombes. Yet Bestombes's view of the war matches very closely that of Bardamu: 'You see, Bardamu, war gives us an incomparable means of testing nervous systems, so it acts as a splendid revealer of the human Spirit!' (P 93 M 89). With this Bardamu agrees, he too believes that war has revealed men's 'Spirit' to him, but where Bestombes sees it as the catalyst of patriotism, and patriotism as the ultimate in noble selflessness, Bardamu sees it as having revealed the human Spirit in all its internecine fury. He is reacting on behalf of those who have fought against a typical civilian justification of the unbearable experience they have been through, and in this reaction there is a solidarity with the large class of those who have 'paid' with their lives, their health, or their happiness. To this extent Bardamu's egotism is humane, because its general acceptance might be taken as likely to lessen the chances of other wars being fought; his mockery of Bestombes is not a mockery of altruism as such, only of altruism put to a wrong use.

Altruism survives as a possibility in the *Journey*, as a human impulse capable of suppressing Bardamu's otherwise universal distrust. There are two altruistic characters in the novel: Molly in Detroit, and sergeant Alcide in colonial Africa. Molly is a stereotype of fiction, the prostitute whose unreflecting kindness belies the venality of her trade and raises her above the common, supposedly more respectable run of humanity. The impression she makes on Bardamu, the lonely foreigner in Detroit, is not so stereotyped, however. She has all the physical buoyancy and easy sexuality he requires of women (especially American women), but the two of them become intimate in 'spirit' as well as in body, so that Bardamu has for her 'an exceptional feeling of trust, which in fearful natures takes the place of love' (P 228 M 206). This is as far emotionally as he is able to go, and as a relation it is one-sided, since he finds and takes comfort from her without making any requital. Molly is not the cure for his solipsism, but he prizes her because she has tried to interest herself in him 'from the inside', to understand his confessed 'egotism'. He is thus spared her adverse judgment on him, and in this she is a person apart.

Molly cannot save Bardamu, then, but in herself she is a conspicuously charitable character. In terms of this novel she is one of those who have 'paid', if voluntarily in her case. Out of her immoral earnings she gives Bardamu the money to buy himself a good suit and then offers to make him an allowance. At the same time she is supporting her younger sister, who is studying in Arizona to be a photographer. This magnanimity at a distance echoes very significantly that of the *Journey*'s other model of altruism, sergeant Alcide, who from his torrid and uncomfortable outpost in West Africa sends money back to Bordeaux for the education of his niece. In Alcide's case the situation is unduly sentimentalised: the girl has been orphaned and has had polio, her uncle is presented as now living in miserable conditions merely so that her chances in life may be improved. The lesson of Alcide is that altruism is made admirable by the degree of suffering that it entails, and the lesson of the two instances together, of Molly and Alcide, is that charity must be exercised at a distance, so bearing out the brutal saying of Bardamu, later in the novel, that 'Being in love's nothing, it's staying together that's difficult.' The fatal obstacle to any such ideal as 'love' is the proximity of other, all too material human bodies. Love Bardamu relegates bitterly to an ideal state of youthfulness, or more tenderly to his memories of Molly, to whom his mind goes back in its rare moments of freedom from egotism, as a woman 'who truly loved men just a little, not just one man, even if it was you, but all' (P 393 M 344).

The young are the proper recipients of charity: Alcide's niece is barely adolescent, Molly's sister still a student – she is learning to be a photographer of birds, which links her with that other class of living creatures for whom Bardamu is prepared to show open sympathy, household animals. Children and pets are alike in their innocence and in deserving far better of the adult world than they get. They are pathetic victims of a general inhumanity. In the grim description which Bardamu gives of the life of the 'backyards' of Clichy, it is first the songbirds in their cages and then the small children of the households that suffer most acutely. The birds are pining away in their unnatural setting and the children are beaten or abused sexually, for the arousal of depraved grown-ups.

Bardamu, ever the voyeur, observes such cruelty but does not try to prevent it.

He does intervene, however, in another case, that of Bébert, the young boy who falls sick of typhoid. The otherwise fatalistic Bardamu becomes by his own admission 'obsessed' with saving this child. He does not in the end save him, but he justifies the fondness which has inspired him to try: 'As long as something's got to be loved, you run less risk with children than with men, you at least have the excuse of hoping they'll be less putrid than us later on' (P 242 M 219). This grudging concession to an ordinary human sympathy is sufficient to persuade Bardamu to cross Paris to the Institut Bioduret, in search of advice from the experts as to how best to help the boy. He can more than tolerate the deaths of grown-ups, he can exult in them, because grown-ups are irredeemably corrupted, but with children it is different, they have a future. We should not perhaps spoil his argument by asking whether the now detestable grown-ups did not once themselves have a future. Little Bébert, however, is already something of a 'visionary', in the line of Robinson and of Bardamu, and already in trouble from the adult world for being so: he masturbates, and his aunt applies to Bardamu for a 'syrup' to cure him of this vice. 'Tell him he'll go mad', is Bardamu's 'classical' advice, which is less classical than it sounds, seeing the virtue he recognises as lying if not in outright madness then in a managed 'delirium'. Bébert is needed in the novel, to lighten the blackness briefly with his smile of 'pure affection'. This 'easy' affection will not last, according to Bardamu, past the age of twenty, which would be late indeed for the terminal point of childhood, but it is the age that Céline himself had reached when he went to war in 1914. Bébert's instinctive affection is one which pet animals too can show; the name of Bébert was later passed on by Céline to his favourite cat.

Bardamu's excursion to the Institut Bioduret affords him one brief refreshment, when he comes to cross the river Seine. Now if the Institut were where the text says that it is, 'behind La Villette', he would have no need to cross the river, because

La Villette would be to the east and not the south of Rancy. Céline is clearly playing with the topography of Paris for a purpose. The crossing of the river is no simple matter for Bardamu, and he hesitates before making it, likening himself to Caesar faced with his decisive passage of the Rubicon. Why the imperial comparison? Because the Seine here is far more than a geographical divide, it is a divide between the real and the unreal, between the awful reality of Rancy and the consoling fantasy that there might be somewhere else where he could live. The river, and the patient fishermen along the banks, are described with an unwonted affection:

The last of the sun kept a nice bit of warmth around us, causing small reflections to dance on the water, blue and gold mixed. A fresh wind was coming from opposite through the tall trees, all smiles the wind, leaning through the thousands of leaves, in soft gusts. It was good there.   (P 288 M 257)

This is not at all the Bardamu we are used to, but a man suddenly and briefly in tune with his surroundings and with his fellow citizens, the idling fishermen along the bank. The river, judging by the meditation it prompts in him, is a boundary between two alternative ways of life, of hurrying blindly on out of youth and into old age, or of letting youth go, with all its 'deceptions' and 'credulity', and settling instead to the contemplation of the truth. Bardamu must return to Rancy. But the river has somehow been a privileged place of repose and companionship for him, as it is a second time, when he visits Toulouse and is entertained, along with Robinson and Madelon, in an episode of rare conviviality on a barge moored to the bank.

Conviviality, however, as well as being rare in the *Journey*, has strict limits. It will not be allowed to evolve into a higher feeling, into a lasting affection. 'There's love, Bardamu', protests Arthur Ganate in the first few pages of the novel, dismayed by his young friend's cynicism; 'Arthur, love is the infinite put within reach of poodles' is the withering reply. And at the far end of the story the notion of romantic love does even worse, leading directly to the final, mortal quarrel between the marriage-seeking Madelon and the furiously independent Robinson. Their proximity is fatal, crammed as they are into a taxi, and Madelon's expectation that Robinson will now take her as his permanent companion proves fatal also. He rejects her not for herself, but on principle: 'I don't want to be loved any more . . . It disgusts me! . . .' In the violent responses he makes to Madelon throughout their lengthy exchange there is a remarkable fear of dependency. And at this, the limit of his perverse career, he abandons his characteristic cynicism in order to declare himself. The cynical and safe course would be to play along with the girl, and make her all the false promises she wants, but Robinson confesses the truth of his inability to love or be loved, and he dies, a martyr to his veracity.

At the dying man's side, Bardamu discovers how far he himself has travelled into the night, away from the compassionate feelings he could have had when young for a human being *in extremis*. He can summon them up no more, and the book's imagery at this demanding moment becomes savagely visceral: 'Such compassion as we had left has been carefully hounded and driven out, like some filthy pill, into the bottom of the body. Compassion's been pushed to the end of our intestines with the shit. Best place for it, we say to ourselves' (P 496 M 434). Compassion can thus only be excreted, it is no longer capable of expression through the mouth, and the voyage which Bardamu has made has effected a terrible reversal in his bodily functions: the good in him will be defecated, and the filth will be spoken. Nevertheless, he is conscious when beside Robinson that he is failing the other in being unable to measure up to the needs of this extreme moment. A more generous, more sympathetic Bardamu might help him to die:

But there was only me, me all right, me alone, beside him, the real Ferdinand who lacked what would make a man bigger than his mere life, a love for the life of others. Of that I had none, or in truth so little that it wasn't worth showing it. I wasn't as big as death.

(P 496 M 435)

Thus Bardamu is not altogether circumscribed by his egotism, he can see beyond it to the nature of the demand that is here being made on him and the nature of the proper response to it. If there is a sadness in the *Journey*, it is this: that his wilful denigration of the world, and of himself, stems from an incapacity to act out his own sympathetic desires.

Chapter 3

Style

The shock that the *Journey* caused when it was first published came as much from the kind of French in which it was written as from the callous philosophy promulgated by Bardamu. Céline's language was not of the polite, educated kind that readers of serious literature in France were accustomed to. Rather, just as Bardamu's philosophy was meant to expose the sham of a received morality, so the register of French it was couched in was meant to overstep the acceptable limits of the literary language. The style of the *Journey* is an integral part of the novelist's assault on values, both ethical and linguistic, that he regarded as false, as embellishing a reality which is in truth far uglier and more venomous than the fine words of traditional prose would have us believe. This was a campaign that Céline launched in the *Journey* and carried on throughout his life, as he worked with increasing obsessiveness to sharpen the idiosyncrasies of his style. His second book, *Death on the Instalment Plan*, is already a great advance in this respect on the *Journey*, so that many admirers of the earlier novel found its verbal mannerisms and difficulties too much for them. The volume in the Pléiade collection that contains the two novels together contains also a forty-page glossary of 'popular and slang vocabulary' presumed by the editor to be unfamiliar to 'normal' French readers; all but a handful of these terms come in the second novel — the *Journey* was written before Céline got fully under way as a virtuoso of 'popular' French.

This is not to say that it is an easy novel, verbally; it is not, it has in it much popular and slang usage that can still come as a shock or a mystery to innocent foreign readers (and which translators have the greatest difficulty in reproducing consistently in their own language). The 'slang' and the

79

'popular' are not to be confused as registers of a language. Slang terms are used in the restricted setting of a trade, a calling, a closed environment of some kind, and tend to the arcane, since outsiders must be initiated in order to know them; 'popular' usage is not arcane, it is the informal register employed every day in speaking by large parts of the population and can generally be understood by those who do not themselves use (and who frequently condemn) it. In the *Journey* Céline employs mainly 'popular' French, not slang; and for good reason. The *argotier*, or user of slang, can not do more than introduce slang terms when they are available: he can not 'write slang' even if it is sometimes claimed that that is what he does, because slang is a vocabulary and not a language, it has no distinctive syntax. As a result the *argotier*'s slang terms stand out as such, isolated amidst the standard language forms around them. Not so 'popular' language; this is genuinely a language, for it has a recognisable vocabulary and syntax of its own.

Céline was not the first writer in France to make use of 'popular' French, but he seems to have been the first ever to try to write in it. In the nineteenth century, Balzac, Victor Hugo, Zola, Jules Vallès, all used 'popular' language-forms for purposes of characterisation, or for bringing it home to bourgeois readers that theirs was not the only kind of French to be found in France. And among Céline's contemporaries, two writers who greatly influenced him, Henri Barbusse and Eugène Dabit, had also used it in their books. But like the *argotiers* with their slang, none of these precursors had done more than *quote* 'popular' language, by setting it into a context of more formal, that is more literary language. In Barbusse's famous anti-war novel, *Le Feu*, for example, the 'popular' usage of the soldiers in the trenches stands out strikingly against the formality of the novel's narrative; it occurs literally between quotation-marks, in dialogue. Céline is the remarkable innovator who did away with the quotation-marks and made this same 'popular' or 'oral' French the idiom in which Bardamu addresses us throughout. The effect on most readers is that of a single, wonderfully graphic and consistent stylistic register, even if under a closer analysis it emerges that Bardamu's French is at many points more classical than we had first suspected. But its overall effect is what counted for Céline's first readers and may still count for us. Nowadays we are no longer so quick to divide language prescriptively into 'correct' and 'incorrect' forms, recognising that so-called 'incorrect' forms are validated by long and widespread use and cannot be looked on as inferior; on the contrary, they may be all the more dramatic and effective for being 'incorrect'. In Céline's day, however, such arguments were not heard: 'correct' usage was synonymous with literary usage. Indeed, it was to literature that prescriptivists naturally looked for their models of correctness. Céline was thus writing as a conscious saboteur, but was dependent for his effectiveness on the continued maintenance by others of the standards he was sabotaging, These standards are now laxer and the style of the *Journey* is not quite the offensive weapon it originally was, though a first exposure to it remains a memorable experience.

This is unquestionably the most resourceful and accomplished of all 'spoken' novels. Its style is that of Bardamu or, more subtly, its style *is* Bardamu, in the sense that the character is a creation of his language, not the other way round (*le barda*, the term used among soldiers in 1914–18 for the equipment they were forced to carry, became emblematic of that patois of the trenches to which after the war survivors looked back with some nostalgia; it has a metaphorical use still in popular French for any gross encumbrance). That style is demotic or, as Céline would like us to think, not a 'style' at all, since 'style' in the honorific sense he looked on as a false adornment, requiring to be forcibly stripped away if the horrors of reality were to be faithfully exposed. Bardamu's is if anything an 'anti-style', the style that will put an end to 'style'.

Its polemical intent is brought vigorously out when he is led to buy a copy of Montaigne's essays from a riverside *bouquiniste* (in the course of the crucial episode of crossing the river discussed earlier). The book costs him just one franc, a laughable price which already hints at the vandalism to come. In it Bardamu at once finds a passage in which the essayist is trying to console his wife for the recent death of one of their children (Bardamu is faced at this point with the loss of Bébert), and does so by sending her a translation of a consolatory passage taken from the Roman moralist, Plutarch. But Bardamu's reported version of Montaigne's words is somewhat less magisterial than the original: 'Come, don't take on, my dear wife! You really must console yourself! . . . It'll work out! . . . Everything works out in life . . .' (P 289 M 258). There is bitterness in this travesty, for stoicism in the face of affliction is not Bardamu's way as it was Montaigne's, and his 'translation' of Montaigne is accordingly altogether less true than Montaigne's no doubt was to Plutarch. The sixteenth-century text has been brutally transposed into a twentieth-century demotic in order to show up its intolerable hollowness. Montaigne has tried, not even in his own words but in those of a classical model, to take the sting out of the death of a child; Bardamu will put the sting back, and in his own words.

The insolently 'popular' tone of Bardamu's voice is fixed in the novel's first few words: 'Ça a débuté comme ça. Moi, j'avais jamais rien dit. Rien.' In 1932, this was not how novels in French were supposed to start; even today, a novel starting similarly might well be thought to be imitating Céline. The words are shocking for being not quoted, but the start of a narrative, and their syntax is that not of books but of the streets. The contraction *ça* in itself, for the correct *cela*, did not then belong in literature, except in dialogue, and to use it twice, at the beginning and the end of one very short inaugural sentence was provocative. The two *ça*s do not have the same grammatical function. The first one is pronominal and stands in an offhand fashion for the narrative of events to come − it is anticipatory where such a pronoun is more properly used to refer back to some concept already expressed; while the second *ça* is adverbial, as part of the equally offhand and in this instance equally anticipatory locution *comme ça*. The quick repetition of this one small word in two different functions shows how economical 'popular' usage can be in its means of expression. Nor should an orthodox narrative in French begin with a verb in the *passé composé*, as with *a débuté*, a 'progressive' past tense which, in distinction from the past historic, establishes a closer intimacy between the moment of narration and the events of the narrative. In the second sentence the same effect of brevity – and paradoxically, seeing what a voluble book this turns out to be, of the laconic – is endorsed. The emphatic *moi* at the start imposes a particular intonation on the words that follow, while the omission of *ne* from in front of the verb goes further towards establishing that this is French as spoken (or heard), not French as written – to be exact, that this is the written version of spoken French, since French as actually spoken may not be reproducible at all. The text's third sentence consists of only the one word *rien*, acceptable as such were it the answer to a question but not, in 1932, in its role of draconian reinforcement as here. In its isolation *rien* seems to speak for the negativity of Bardamu's whole philosophy.

These three opening sentences contain eleven words in all, and with a single exception extremely plain words. The exception is *débuté*, which is almost ornate in the circumstances; one might have expected Bardamu to use the plainer *commencé* – *débuté* is an early sign that he is more ambitious lexically than he perhaps ought to be. The sentences are very deliberately short and crude, but they are not clumsy. Céline in fact had a remarkable ear for the rhythms of French prose. He was admiring of what was referred to at the time as the 'syncopation' of written language (by analogy with the syncopation of jazz and other modern music), and as his own style matures in his later books its artfully broken rhythms become more and more insistent. But even in these simple opening notes of the *Journey* it is possible to hear a certain 'music', and to know that Bardamu's spoken French will be a very much more carefully arranged form of it than any to be heard in public places.

An adequate translation of the *Journey* needs to find a

homogeneous register in its own language capable of preserving the novel's thousands of 'popular' forms. English, alas, seems not to yield one. Manheim's translation of the *Journey* opens: 'Here's how it started. I'd never said a word. Not one word'. *Here's* for *here is*, and *I'd* for *I had*, are still recognised to be colloquial rather than standard written forms even in 1989, but only just, and overall Manheim's three sentences are more 'grammatical' than Céline's. There is nothing in the English to match the repetition of *ça*, nor the omission of *ne*, nor the emphatic use of *moi, j'*. A stronger impersonation of Bardamu's voice here might go: 'It was like this it began. Me, I'd not uttered. Not a word', in which there are at least comparable vulgarisms. Bardamu is a narrator who, in linguistic as well as social terms, goes slumming, he is a bourgeois who has taken it on himself to speak the idiom of the *miteux*; for a translator that is a hard, I suspect an impossible act to follow.

In order to identify some of the commoner items of 'popular' French usage which Céline introduces into the novel, I will take a paragraph more or less at random from the same episode in which Bardamu is sold a cheap copy of Montaigne:

Les bouquinistes des quais fermaient leurs boîtes. "Tu viens!" que criait la femme par-dessus le parapet à son mari, à mon côté, qui refermait lui ses instruments, et son pliant et les asticots. Il a grogné et tous les autres pêcheurs ont grogné après lui et on est remontés, moi aussi, là-haut, en grognant, avec les gens qui marchent. Je lui ai parlé à sa femme, comme ça pour lui dire quelque chose d'aimable avant que ça soye la nuit partout. Tout de suite, elle a voulu me vendre un livre. C'en était un de livre qu'elle avait oublié de rentrer dans sa boîte à ce qu'elle prétendait. "Alors ce serait pour moins cher, pour presque rien . . ." qu'elle ajoutait. Un vieux petit "Montaigne" un vrai de vrai pour un franc. Je voulais bien lui faire plaisir à cette femme pour si peu d'argent. Je l'ai pris son Montaigne.

(P 288–9 M 258)

Literary French has evolved since Céline's day, but there are things here forever unacceptable to it. In the second sentence the *que* following the words quoted and preceding the verb is redundant, it has no grammatical function; if it is used in speaking it is for elocutionary, or else rhythmic purposes. From a 'literary' standpoint, this same sentence is vulgar in its repetitions, *à son mari* with *à mon côté*, *et son pliant* with *et les asticots*, but its rhythm is compelling and serves to give prominence to the *asticots* (maggots), creatures beloved of Céline but here temporarily paroled from their more sinister posthumous duties. The fourth sentence has a redundant *lui*, in *Je lui ai parlé à sa femme*, unless we take it to be an ethical dative, referring to the husband, rather than a pronoun anticipating the indirect object *sa femme*. The same sentence ends as much curiously as incorrectly, *avant que ça soye la nuit partout*. Here, the casual *ça* becomes the subject of a verb (*être*) which is in the present subjunctive and spelt sardonically in an archaic form − *soye* for *soit* − as if Bardamu could never seriously condone so stilted a verb-form. Correct French at this point would have: 'avant qu'il ne fasse nuit partout'. There are further syntactical solecisms: *C'en était un de livre* [. . .], *Alors ce serait pour moins cher* [. . .], both of which are intended as representations of the bookseller's own ill-formed words − in the first example their status as narrated speech is belatedly indicated by the phrase *à ce qu'elle prétendait*. Before the paragraph ends, we have a second redundant *que*, and two more duplications of objects with verbs, one indirect, *lui* [. . .] *à cette femme*, the other direct *l'* [. . .] *son 'Montaigne'*. The solecism-count in these few lines is in fact extraordinarily high; too high, it might be thought, giving grounds for the complaint that Céline often overdoes things. (It would be wasteful to give the Manheim translation of this passage; it contains not a single departure from an orthodox written English).

So much for Bardamu's syntax, His vocabulary too could daunt a translator, even if in the *Journey* Céline is much less inventive lexically than he was to become later on. In his œuvre as a whole, he is calculated to have coined a thousand verbs, two thousand adjectives and a comparable number of nouns not to be found in any dictionary of French (see Godard: 1985, p 100). In this early book, however, he is content to introduce existing terms from slang and 'popular' French, rather than making up exuberant new ones of his own. The best place to look for such terms is in passages of direct speech, for despite the remarkable colloquialism of Bardamu's narration, it remains recognisably more formal in its language than the explicit dialogue. And of all the characters, the slangiest is Robinson. He, the archetypal *révolté*, is logically enough the embodiment also of *argot*, an idiom, as Céline once defined it, by which the *miteux* can take revenge for the insults of deprivation. *Argot* is the language that enables 'the worker to tell his boss he loathes him [. . .]' Robinson is a good deal more savage in his talk than is Bardamu, and is himself of the class of narrator, recalling his past with a virulence clearly felt by him as compensation for the humiliations he has known.

Here he is telling Bardamu how he came to flee from Toulouse, where he has been living with Madelon and her mother:

. . .Tout de même de les entendre discuter comme ça là-dessus pendant des heures ça me donnait mal au ventre! La colique! Je sais bien à quoi ça sert les femmes tout de même! Toi aussi hein? A rien! J'ai voyagé quand même! Un soir enfin qu'elles m'avaient mis bien à bout avec leurs salades, j'ai fini par lui balancer d'un coup à la mère tout ce que je pensais d'elle! "Vous êtes qu'une vieille noix, que je lui ai dit . . . Vous êtes encore plus con que la mère Henrouille! . . . Si vous aviez connu un peu plus de gens et des pays comme j'en ai connu moi vous iriez pas si vite à donner des conseils à tout le monde et c'est toujours pas en ramassant vos bouts de suif dans le coin de votre dégueulasse d'église que vous l'apprendrez jamais la vie! Sortez donc un peu aussi vous ça vous fera du bien! Allez donc vous promener un peu vieille ordure! Ça vous rafraîchira! Vous aurez moins de temps pour faire des prières, vous sentirez moins la vache! . . .   (P 453 M 396–7)

The grammar here, as one would expect, is not good; but I will ignore that and pick out instead the items of slang or 'popular' vocabulary that Robinson uses: *salades* first of all, meaning something like our own contemporary 'garbage': *balancer* as used here, to mean 'let someone have it'; *noix* and *ordure*, as insulting forms of address, equivalent to 'moron' and 'shitheap'; and finally *con* ('bloody stupid') and *dégueulasse* ('lousy'), both of which are more widely used now than fifty years ago but still marked 'F' for 'familiar' in dictionaries of French. In its venom Robinson's outburst illustrates very well the vindictive role that Céline attributes to *argot*: Robinson is using it to defend himself against encroachment by a potential family, to reassert his autonomy (though what we read is what Robinson *says* he said, we have still to decide whether his tirade may not be a form of vengeful *esprit d'escalier*).

As for the rhythm of such a passage: one would like to say that it is the rhythm of speech, of prose broken up into stressed, mainly short units, with marked pauses for the speaker to draw breath. But this is the rhythm of speech as we imagine it, not as we hear it; Céline is not reproducing French speech patterns, he is creating them. Such was his concern to make his prose sound good that, according to his regular typist, whenever he wanted to change what he had written he would beat time as he did so to ensure that the 'music' was not lost. Rhythm in prose turns a great deal on punctuation, since it is through stops and commas that it is controlled, that the breath-groups can be extended or shortened, and above all varied. To the conventional marks of punctuation Céline added one of his own, his 'three dots', of which there are three examples in the speech of Robinson's quoted above. He did not invent these, because they already existed in French, as '*points de suspension*', and they relate to that figure of classical rhetoric known as aposiopesis, whereby a sentence is broken off before its appointed time, and left to be completed by its hearer or reader; aposiopesis is a figure of complicity between interlocutors. But Céline, predictably, diverts the *points de suspension* from their traditional use. Far from being left unfinished, his sentences are peculiarly complete, consisting as they do of a single strident clause. Indeed, he uses his three dots for an opposite purpose, of furthering the independence and hence the impact of each sentence. Read out loud, Céline's prose is syncopated very distinctively by these marked intervals. Even when we are reading it silently we cannot but notice them, and the tension they set up between the great urgency of individual sentences − often ending in

exclamation-marks — and the managed tempo of their utterance. In his longer, more 'literary' sentences, Céline wat-
ches over the rhythm with equal care. If one reads out loud
the sentence of Robinson's above beginning 'Si vous aviez
connu. . .', which has more than fifty words in it and no
punctuation at all before the concluding exclamation-mark, it
is both easily said and easily understood. Robinson's sentiments may be far from admirable, but we should dwell on and
applaud the literary skill that has gone to their expression. This
is the crowning paradox of a paradoxical novel: *Journey to the
End of the Night* is without question beautifully written.

Chapter 4

Posterity

The first publisher of the *Journey* specified in his blurb who might be drawn to read the book: 'doctors whom the author attacks with particular violence, university teachers, literary people'. He was wrong about the doctors, who did not rise to Céline's bait, wrong too about the university teachers, inasmuch as it took many years for the *Journey* to be admitted to the academic canon in France, but right, if also hardly in danger of being wrong, about the 'literary people', since, as I have tried to show, this is a very literate and elaborate book, whose artistry is obscured only by its vehemence. The publication of the novel was the literary event of the season. But its earliest readers took it to be a political book. So vicious was the representation he had given of twentieth-century life that Céline was widely mistaken for a man of the left, and his novel for a partisan bulletin on the terminal state of Western capitalism. French Communists, eager for literary backing of such quality, saw the *Journey* as taking their side, although the more sceptical of them pointed to an awkward fact: that Céline might not like capitalism but had given no sign of wanting to throw in his lot with the proletariat, nor of looking for some violent reorganisation of society. The novel was ambiguous politically, and its shrewder commentators warned their left-wing readers not to conclude that Céline was a closet revolutionary. The *Journey* was most popular among those who might have called themselves anarchists, the intelligent 'antis' who had no party but were against a great many things in France, and in favour of rather few. To young middle-class intellectuals who had broken furiously with the bourgeoisie that had borne them, Céline seemed to be giving a brave if inimitable lead. The couple who over the next forty years were to be the most formidable and influential intellectual ménage in France, Simone de Beauvoir and Jean-Paul Sartre, were both inspired by his malevolent novel. 'We knew heaps of passages from it by heart', Beauvoir later wrote in her memoirs; 'His anarchism seemed close to our own. He was attacking war, colonialism, mediocrity, clichés, society, in a style and a tone that delighted us.' And Sartre's epochal novel of 1938, *La Nausée*, quotes approvingly on its title-page a line from Céline's play, *L'Eglise*: 'He's a lad of no importance collectively, he's quite simply an individual.' The remark is made of Bardamu, by his enemy, the Jewish League of Nations offical Yudenzweck; and since Céline was entirely on the side of the individual, its implications are anti-semitic. This is ironic, seeing that Sartre, now no longer a passionate individualist but a passionate Party man, attacked Céline scurrilously after 1945 for his anti-semitism, accusing him of having been in the pay of the Nazis, and covered his own use of the lines from *L'Eglise* by explaining that he had not read the play when he quoted from it and so did not know that it was anti-semitic. Nevertheless, he continued to say to the end of his life that the *Journey* was one of the few books that had really counted for him, and that its author was one twentieth-century French writer sure to enter literary history.

Céline did not last very long as a presumed crypto-communist. In 1936 he visited Soviet Russia, where the *Journey* had been translated (and bowdlerised in the process), and when he came back he wrote a brief but dismissive pamphlet on the country, where he had been disgusted above all by the optimism of its official ideology. And once he had published the first of his major pamphlets, *Bagatelles pour un massacre*, it was clear to everyone that if he belonged anywhere politically it was on the far right, among the fascists, the monarchists and the anti-semites. But the far right never wholly trusted Céline either, for so rabid was he in the charges that he made, against the Jews and against a good many other innocuous classes of person, that they suspected he was not serious, but a buffoon association with whom might imperil their own more practical political cause. Rather, the forever unclubbable Céline was committed to what, in *Semmelweis*, he had called 'the sonorities of impotence'. He seems genuinely to have believed that his propaganda was quite without effect in the real world, and that he could write anything he liked, however irresponsible. Even after the war, and in the full knowledge of what anti-semitism had turned into in practice, he admitted to no connection between the demented, fulminating pamphlets he had published in the 1930s and the monstrous genocide of the Nazis.

But he had suffered ignominy, and after the war it was hardly possible for anyone in France to claim Céline for literature. He was stigmatised as a collaborator, or, since there was no real evidence of that, as a Nazi sympathiser, and held to have well deserved the punishment he had been given. His literary reputation and influence, high indeed after the publication of his first two novels, were in abeyance. There were some who supported him, however, and in 1949, while he was still an exile in Denmark, a new edition of the *Journey* was published. For it Céline wrote a preface, in which he sought to deflect the hostility felt against him, as he well knew, for his pamphlets on to the novel − 'The one truly malicious book out of all my books [. . .]' No one will have been taken in by this, but such a disingenuous attempt at his exculpation does reveal how deeply Céline's reputation as a writer had been compromised by his political passions. That reputation was slowly restored during the 1950s, by which time he was back in France, not yet forgiven but at least tolerated, and publishing afresh. Before he died the decision had been made to bring out his two great pre-war novels, the *Journey* and *Death on the Instalment Plan*, in the canonical Bibliothèque de la Pléïade. Céline himself crowed, knowing that he was only the second living French writer to have been so honoured. The volume appeared in 1962, a year after his death, but it may be taken as the definitive act in his literary restitution.

In the nearly thirty years since then, Céline's literary heirs have had time to declare themselves, but there have, in a direct sense, been none,. This is not surprising, because he is far too strong and distinctive a writer ever to attract close followers. No one could be more likely to instil in other writers Harold Bloom's famous 'anxiety of influence', whereby those most readily captivated by his œuvre would fight the hardest to break free from its influence. Moreover, he became so very idiosyncratic in his later writings that few if any French writers will have had the verbal capacity to try and imitate him. But the fact that he has had no identifiable heirs − the one exception is not French: the American writer Henry Miller was an avowed devotee of the early Céline and hugely influenced by him in the writing of such novels as *Tropic of Cancer* − does not mean that he has not helped to shape French writing since the war. He very clearly has, and above all as the author of the *Journey*, for this is the most imposing and accessible of his books. Its influence has been of the most telling kind, not localised but diffuse; for the novel embodies in a concentrated and uniquely vivid form tendencies in literature that have flourished greatly in the West since 1945.

It showed the way first, for an extension of the legitimate subject-matter of fiction, into those places and practices in society which novelists had earlier done no more than flirt with, either because they knew too little about them or because they respected current taboos on their invocation. Céline was not the first writer to describe, or to imagine, the ultimate abjection of poor urban lives or the bestialities of war or of colonialism, but no one before him had presented them with the same force or the same cynicism, as if these were awful facts of modern life about which there was nothing to be done. The *Journey* looks ahead to the considerable Western literature of alienation, in which human beings are shown as both the degraded product and the victims of their egotistical modern societies. And then, for a novel published early in the 1930s, it is unprecedently forward in the place that it gives to sexuality and daringly nonchalant in introducing such more or less forbidden topics as abortion, masturbation, or child abuse. Here too it was a precursor, of that obsession of postwar fiction with the varieties of sexual experience and of that now familiar, gloating materialism which sees biology as the one certain determinant of human life. The *Journey* is prophetic also in its psychoanalytical aspect. I have said that Céline was no professional Freudian, but he took over from Freud the (to him auspicious) idea that the subconscious mind is a far murkier place than the conscious one, and that human societies survive only through the systematic repression of our innate hostility to one another; in Freudian terms, the voice of Bardamu in the *Journey* is the 'return of the repressed', revealing to us the previously censored truth of our condition. But the morbidity of such a vision as Céline's no longer seems so pathological and offensive as it did in 1932, for we have grown, as we believe, more lucid in these respects, and less inclined to harbour idealisms.

If, thematically, the *Journey* is almost a compendium of postwar fiction, then in its style it is more modern still, having done more than any other single piece of writing in French to break up the old hegemony of the 'literary' language. It did this by effecting a radical shift in the writing of fiction, away from narrative and towards narration. That is, by seeming to be 'spoken' to us by Bardamu, the novel enacts the actual telling of a story, and it is only through this telling that we have any knowledge of the 'told'. There is no pretence in the *Journey* that Bardamu is a historian, recounting what is objectively true and what others beside himself might have recounted similarly; he is a story-teller, in the full ambiguity of that English term, and we cannot look on him as altogether or even mainly reliable in what he says. With such a narration we enter into what has been called (by Nathalie Sarraute first of all) 'the age of suspicion' in literature, in which novelists abandon their ancient claim to certainty as to the facts of their narrative and deliver us up instead to the uncertainties of the active imagination. Céline is a writer rare for the immediacy and violence of his imagination, and as such one of the great progenitors of self-conscious fiction. In the years since his death literary history has gone his way, so that this, his first, most traditional and morally most offensive novel now seems to us a tamer book than it should, because it is in such close keeping, in subject as well as method, with so much later writing. It stands nevertheless as one of the masterworks of the modern literature of pessimism, which is as much as to say, as one of the landmarks of our own enduringly pessimistic age.

Guide to further reading

The *Journey* is by no means the whole of Céline, and the best reading anyone could do as a sequel to it is of others of his own books. His second novel of 1936, *Mort à crédit*, is more exotic and hence more difficult in its language than the *Journey*, but it is a very powerful, bawdy, and embattled book, concerned with experiences of childhood and adolescence such as are notably missing from the earlier novel. It has been translated twice into English as *Death on the Instalment Plan*; the better translation to read is Ralph Manheim's (1966). Similarly, two of the books which Céline published after the war: *D'Un château l'autre* (1957) and *Nord* (1960), contain tremendous, apocalyptic recreations of Nazi Germany in its final collapse, as does a third, rather lesser volume, *Rigodon* (1969), on which the novelist was still working when he died. This trilogy now forms a second volume of Céline's writings in the Bibliothèque de la Pléïade (Gallimard, 1974), and passable translations of its component books have been made by Ralph Manheim: *Castle to Castle* (1969), *North* (1972) and *Rigodon* (1975). (All three of these translations were reissued by Penguin, but at the time of writing in April 1989 all three were out of print.) Although they are certainly not the equal of Céline's best work, his two novels set in London during the First World War, *Guignol's Band* (1944) and its continuation, *Le Pont de Londres* (1964), have their moments and are intriguing for English readers for giving a wild, very Célinian picture of the low life of London in 1915–16 (the two books, together with *Casse-Pipe*, a surviving fragment of an 'army' novel which Céline began writing in 1936–7 but then abandoned, now form a third Pléïade volume of his writings, Gallimard, 1988). *Guignol's Band* exists in English, in a lively translation by Bernard Frechtman and Jack T. Nile (Vision Press, 1954)

The literature on Céline is large, and growing year by year. The *Journey* at least has become a set text in literature courses, both in France and abroad, and academics in a number of countries have published extensively on him. However, most of the worthwhile secondary literature has so far been written in French.

First, as to Céline's life. Two full biographies have appeared to date, both of them in French and both of merit. The first, in three volumes, is by François Gibault (Mercure de France, 1977–85); the second, in a single large volume, by Frédéric Vitoux (Grasset, 1988). Vitoux is the more stylish, economical and thoughtful writer of the two, and his biography adds something to Gibault's by bringing in more evidence about Céline's last years from his widow, Lucette Almansor. An incomparable biographical resource which appeared in the years following Céline's death is the two issues of *Cahiers de l'Herne*, edited by Dominique de Roux (No 3, 1963, and No 5, 1965). These contain memories of Céline by his friends and others, essays on his work, lost or unpublished texts by him and some of his correspondence. These two *Cahiers* were combined into a single volume and republished in 1972. A series of *Cahiers Céline* has also been appearing (from Gallimard) since 1976, which has published very interesting documents by and about the writer, including more of his impassioned correspondence.

Of the literary studies of Céline published in French, all but a very few are for specialists. His biographer, Frédéric Vitoux, is the author of two other commendable books: a textual study, *Louis-Ferdinand Céline: Misère et parole* (Gallimard, 1973), and a long essay ostensibly about the novelist's celebrated pet, *Bébert: le chat de Louis-Ferdinand Céline* (Grasset, 1976), in which Vitoux uses the animal as an oblique and revealing excuse for studying the attitudes of its owner. The most instructive single essay on the *Journey* is that by the 'thematic' critic Jean-Pierre Richard, *La Nausée de Céline* (Fata Morgana, 1973), which traces the powerful imagery of collapse and deliquescence in the text of the novel. The most informed and thorough of all French critics of

Céline is Henri Godard, his editor in the Bibliothèque de la Pléïade. Godard's notes to the *Journey* in the relevant Pléïade volume (Gallimard, 1981; this replaces absolutely the earlier, 1962, Pléïade Céline, which had little or no apparatus) are extremely full, pertinent and well organised, and I have drawn on them very gratefully in my own essay. Godard is also the author of what is far and away the most detailed and authoritative study yet of Céline's language, *Poétique de Céline* (Gallimard, 1985). A useful anthology of French criticism has been produced by Jean-Pierre Dauphin: *Les Critiques de notre temps et Céline* (Garnier, 1976).

Of the books written in English on Céline, the most balanced and accessible is that by Patrick McCarthy, *Céline* (Allen Lane, 1975). McCarthy calls his book a 'critical biography', and it deals briskly and sensibly with the combustible issues of the writer's anti-semitism and wartime activities. Of real interest as the work of an American (Jewish) academic who got to know Céline and corresponded with him is Milton Hindus, *The Crippled Giant* (1950; new, expanded edition, University Press of New England, 1986), which contains Hindus's recollections of the writer and copies of the letters they exchanged. Two other studies, more purely academic, are: Nicholas Hewitt, *The Golden Age of Louis-Ferdinand Céline* (Atlanta, GA, Berg, 1987), which investigates the nostalgic aspects of Céline and sets some of his preoccupations − e.g., over public health − in a historical context; and Ian Noble, *Language and Narration in Céline's Writings* (Macmillan, 1987), which concentrates on him as a technician or master of verbal persuasion. Both these books have ambitious, intelligent points to make. Finally, as a brief, clear and mature essay on the writer: David Hayman, *Louis-Ferdinand Céline*, a pamphlet first published in 1965 (Columbia University Press).